Ephesians

Ephesians

GEOFFREY B. WILSON

MINISTER OF BIRKBY BAPTIST CHURCH
HUDDERSFIELD

THE BANNER OF TRUTH TRUST

THE BANNER OF TRUTH TRUST
3 Murrayfield Road, Edinburgh EH12 6EL
P.O. Box 621, Carlisle, Pennsylvania 17013, USA

*

© Geoffrey Backhouse Wilson
First published 1978
ISBN 0 85151 263 1

*

Printed in Great Britain by
Hazell Watson & Viney Ltd
Aylesbury, Bucks

With gratitude to God
for the life of
JOSEPH WEBSTER BACKHOUSE
of Liverpool,
Corn Merchant and Preacher of the Gospel,
1873–1929.

CONTENTS

PREFACE   9

INTRODUCTION   11

CHAPTER ONE   15

CHAPTER TWO   42

CHAPTER THREE   62

CHAPTER FOUR   79

CHAPTER FIVE   103

CHAPTER SIX   123

BIBLIOGRAPHY   140

PREFACE

My debt both to the past and the present will be evident from a glance at the list of books consulted, and I am glad of this opportunity to thank the authors and publishers who have kindly given permission to quote from their works. I am grateful to the staff of Dr Williams's Library and New College Library for the loan of a number of elusive books on Ephesians.

In preparing the work for the press I have profited from the advice and helpful suggestions of the publishers on several points. The commentary is based on the American Standard Version (1901), published by Thomas Nelson Inc., New Jersey.

Huddersfield,   GEOFFREY WILSON
January 1978

INTRODUCTION

Of the four Epistles which date from Paul's first imprisonment in Rome, Ephesians, Colossians, and Philemon bear the marks of having been written at about the same time, while Philippians is probably best placed near the end of that period of captivity. Ephesians is the most majestic of Paul's letters, but because it is also the most general and least personal of them, not a few have questioned its authenticity. Such scepticism fails to recognize that a change of purpose can account for an author's change of style. Specific problems are dealt with in Colossians and Philemon, but Ephesians contains no hint that the apostle has any particular situation in mind. Yet even the vagueness of its temporal setting serves to enhance its universal appeal, as Paul here gratefully contemplates all things in the light of God's eternal election. Moreover, his sustained use of the language of exalted praise is admirably adapted to the sublime unfolding of its lofty theme – the glorious destiny which belongs to the church in virtue of her union with Christ.

Those who deny the apostolic authorship not only fly in the face of the great weight of evidence that supports it, but are also bound to maintain that an unknown imitator of greater genius than his supposed model was successful in foisting a 'pious' forgery upon a church which was famous for its spiritual discernment [Rev 2.2]. And though much has been made of the fact that in Colossians there are close links with no less than 78 of this Epistle's 155 verses, these ideas are not reproduced in any mechanical fashion as would be the case with a mere forger, but they receive the fresh development which only their originator could give to them.

The absence of the words 'at Ephesus' from the best manuscripts is probably an indication that Paul intended the Epistle to be read by a group of churches around Ephesus. This 'circular letter' theory also explains the verses which imply that the writer and readers have not met [1.15; 3.2, 4], and the omission of any personal greetings. It therefore seems likely that 'Ephesians' is the letter 'from Laodicea' to which the apostle refers in Col 4.16.

Paul was prompted to write these two great 'Prison Epistles' by the disturbing news Epaphras had brought to him of the situation in Colosse, where the rise of a heresy which dethroned Christ and denied the sufficiency of his work threatened to overthrow the faith throughout the Lycus Valley [Col 2.8ff]. As a good physician of souls Paul sent the right antidote to counteract the poison of error (Colossians), and the right tonic to build up the faith of all believers in Asia Minor (Ephesians). Tychicus, who was entrusted with both letters, evidently took the encyclical to the churches where it was to be read [6.21; Col 4.7]. Probably the address was left blank in the original letter, so that this could be orally filled in by the reader at each particular place.

It was Paul's refusal to discriminate against Gentiles in favour of Jews which had brought him to Rome 'as the prisoner of Jesus Christ' [3.1; cf Acts 21.17ff; 22.21–24], and in this Epistle he explains the once secret but now revealed mystery of the unity of Jews and Gentiles in the one body of Christ [2.11ff; 3.2ff]. This unity was the purchase of Christ's blood, whose death broke down the dividing wall of the legal economy and so made peace between them [2.14, 15].

Thus it is in the apostle's exposition of the essential meaning of the New Covenant, both in its blessings [ch 1–3] and its duties [ch 4–6], that we have his spiritual testament to the church. It is the charter which teaches us that the church is the society of the future, for as the Bride of Christ it is the one society to which the future belongs.

CHAPTER ONE

After greeting his readers [vv 1, 2], Paul bursts into a great thanksgiving to God for all the blessings of salvation in Christ – election, redemption, and the assurance of the promised inheritance through the gift of the Holy Spirit [vv 3–14]. The opening doxology thus strikes the note of adoring worship which is evident throughout the first half of the Epistle. This praise is followed by the apostle's prayer for further spiritual blessings. He is thankful for their faith and love, but he prays for increased wisdom and understanding to enable them to realize that the power of God at work in them is the same power which raised Christ from the dead and made him the Head of the church which is his body [vv 15–23].

V1 : Paul, an apostle of Christ Jesus through the will of God, to the saints that are at Ephesus, and the faithful in Christ Jesus:

It is important to note that the abiding significance of all that follows is determined by the validity of Paul's opening appeal to the fact of his apostleship. He is conscious that his words possess unique authority for the whole church of God, because he knows that he is 'an apostle of Christ Jesus through the will of God.' The word 'apostle' (or 'sent one') connects the one who is sent (Paul) with the Sender (Christ) and thus draws attention to the special charge which authorizes the mission; whereas the ordinary Greek word for 'send' merely links the sender with the recipient (K. Rengstorf, *Theological Dictionary of the New Testament*, Vol. I, p. 398). What Paul claims is that the grace of apostleship was conferred upon him through the initiative of God and the direct call of Christ. And it was the *personal* appearance of the Risen Lord to Paul which transformed the persecutor into a *witness* who was now *sent forth* to preach the very gospel he had tried to overthrow [cf *Acts* 26.16, 17: 'unto whom I send (*apostellō*) thee']. 'From this it appears clearly how the Sovereign Lord himself changed, called and appointed Paul to be his "apostle" in the fullest sense of the word – one clothed with the authority and endued with the power of his Sender, to go forth and act as his representative in the fulfilling of the commission given to him' (J. Norval Geldenhuys, *Supreme Authority*, p. 63).

As already noted in the Introduction, the traditional view that this Epistle was the peculiar property of the Ephesian church cannot be sustained by the evidence, which rather points to its wider circulation among the churches around Ephesus. Yet even though Ephesus was not the Epistle's only destination, it is better to retain the words 'at Ephesus' than to omit them, as does the RSV, because this message was sent to Christians living in particular places. For the church of Christ would be nothing more than a vague idea without its visible manifestation in definite localities. But instead of using the term 'church,' Paul here chooses to remind his readers of the dignity and duty that is theirs as 'the saints' and 'faithful' who are 'in Christ Jesus.' The root of both designations is found in Israel's consecration and consequent calling to faithful service [*Exod* 19.5, 6]. As Israel was brought into the sphere of covenant blessing to obey God's commands [*Lev* 19.2], so the new Israel of God has now been chosen to serve him in holiness of heart and life [cf 1 *Pet* 2.9 where *Israel's* distinctive titles are transferred to the *church*; *Rom* 6.22; 2 *Cor* 7.1].

Such obedience is possible only because they are 'in Christ Jesus,' who is not only their personal Saviour but also the

Head of this new community, into which they have been incorporated by grace. It is not too much to say that the whole
of Paul's experience and teaching of Christ is summed up in
the phrase 'in Christ Jesus,' upon which the Epistle itself is but
one large comment. The key to its meaning is found in
Christ as the Head of the new creation through his redemptive
achievement as the second Adam [note that the first time 'in
Christ' occurs in *Romans* is in 6.11, following the teaching of
Rom 5.12–21]. Thus a corporate relationship is here in view,
for our individual salvation in Christ also makes us members
of the church which is his body [1.23; 2.15]. Truly, 'the New
Testament knows nothing of a solitary Christianity' (John
Wesley).

V2: **Grace to you and peace from God our Father and
the Lord Jesus Christ.**

As in all Paul's Epistles the conventional greeting is replaced
by the prayer that those who read his words may be enriched
with the twin blessings of 'grace' [1.6, 7; 2.5, 7, 8; 3.2, 7, 8;
4.7, 29; 6.24] and 'peace' [2.14, 15, 17; 4.3; 6.15, 23]. He
wants them to enjoy the free favour of God in Christ and the
deep peace which flows from it. In an Epistle which dwells
upon the essential unity of all believers in Christ, this combi-
nation of Greek and Jewish forms of greeting is especially
appropriate. The linking together of the Father and the Son
under a single preposition ('from') evidently assumes their
complete equality. While it would be a startling offence to
associate the name of the greatest reformer, saint, or even
apostle with the name of God in this way, there is one reason
why it is not blasphemous to speak of God and Christ as the
joint-bestowers of all grace and peace to men. It is because
'Jesus Christ is God. Being God, and for that reason only, he
can be linked in this stupendous fashion with God the Father
and can be separated from the whole universe of created

things' (J. Gresham Machen, *The Christian Faith in the Modern World*, p. 224).

V3 : Blessed *be* the God and Father of our Lord Jesus Christ, who hath blessed us with every spiritual blessing in the heavenly *places* in Christ;

The stately elevated style of Ephesians is due to the fact that most of the apostle's teaching in this Epistle, particularly in the first three chapters, is expressed in the language of prayer. Although the long opening doxology [*vv* 3–14], recalls the form of the Jewish *berakah* (blessing), it has a distinctively Christian content. In three stanzas of unequal length, Paul here gratefully surveys the grace of God in our salvation, as he progressively describes the work of the Father [*vv* 3–6], Son [*vv* 7–12], and Holy Spirit [*vv* 13–14], punctuating each section with a phrase that points to the glory of the Father's sovereign initiative [*vv* 6, 12, 14].

Blessed *be* This first word of heartfelt praise strikes the keynote of Paul's great thanksgiving. As the absolutely 'blessed' (*eulogētos*) One, God is infinitely worthy of that ascriptive praise which acknowledges him as the sole source of every blessing, even though it can add nothing to his essential blessedness [cf *Luke* 1.68; *2 Cor* 1.3; *1 Pet* 1.3]. For while God blesses us by his *deeds of grace* ('with every spiritual blessing'), we can only bless him by our *words of gratitude*.

the God and Father of our Lord Jesus Christ, This single mention of the name of God shows that he is the subject of the entire sentence [*vv* 3–14]. God is from eternity the *Father* of the Son, but it was not until the Word was made flesh for our salvation that he also became his *God* [*John* 20.17]. And we are taught here to bless God for this provision of his grace, because it is only through the merits of *our* Mediator that we are brought to know God as *our* Father [cf *v* 5: 'having fore-ordained us unto *adoption as sons* through Jesus Christ unto himself'].

who hath blessed us Or rather 'who blessed us,' the aorist tense pointing to the time when God called us to faith in Christ, an event which the 'even as' of verse 4 traces back to our election. The idea 'is that in calling us to Christian faith God blessed us, and that the great deed of blessing which thus took effect in time had its foundation in an eternal election' (S. D. F. Salmond). Consequently no one ever becomes a believer by the power of his own choice [*John* 1.13], but only because the Father draws him to Christ [*John* 6.44].

with every spiritual blessing The nature of God's decisive act of 'blessing' is here described. This includes 'every *spiritual* blessing' [cf 5.19], i.e. all those blessings that are brought by the Spirit, and that lead to life in the Spirit [*vv* 13, 14; *Rom* 8.1–27; *Gal* 4.6; 5.22–23]. 'All, and yet but one blessing; to note that spiritual blessings are so knit together, that they all make up but one blessing; and where God gives one, he gives all' (John Trapp).

in the heavenly *places* in Christ: Union with Christ has made the believer an inhabitant of two worlds. Spiritually he is already raised and seated with Christ 'in the heavenly places' [2.6], though meanwhile he lives in the body on earth as a stranger and pilgrim whose true citizenship is in heaven [*Phil* 3.20; *Heb* 11.13]. Paul's use of the phrase here shows that these spiritual blessings have their origin in heaven, and it is from heaven that our enthroned Head [1.20] dispenses this largesse to his members on earth. Thus we are blessed by God because we are 'in Christ.' The blessings have their source in our election 'in Christ,' and they were secured for us by his death; but they become ours in actual possession only in virtue of our vital union with him.

*V*4: **even as he chose us in him before the foundation of the world, that we should be holy and without blemish before him in love:**

even as he chose us This presents election as the sole ground of all the blessings vouchsafed to believers. It was not that they chose God, for they became believers only because God first chose them. The verb 'chose' '*always* has, and must *of logical necessity* have, a reference to others to whom the chosen would, without the *choosing out*, still belong' (H. A. W. Meyer). And it was from the mass of fallen humanity that God chose out *for himself* (middle voice) a people whom he formed to show forth his praise [*Is* 43.21; 1 *Pet* 2.9,10]. In the divine decree which contemplated the race as ruined by the fall, God thus chose to save some to the praise of his mercy, while leaving the non-elect to suffer the consequences of their sin to the praise of his justice [*Rom* 9.17–23]. 'Us' joins Paul with his readers, and it expresses the apostle's adoring wonder at the inscrutability of God's choice, unprompted as it is by any foreseen merit in those so chosen to receive an eternal inheritance [*Rom* 9.11, 13, 16].

in him The brief phrase conveys a vital truth, for it was only in their worthy Redeemer that such a choice of the unworthy could be made. God's election, says Calvin, is like 'a registering of us in writing' in which 'Jesus Christ serves as a register. It is in him that we are written down and acknowledged by God as his children. Seeing, then, that God had an eye to us in the person of Jesus Christ, it follows that he did not find anything in us which we might lay before him to cause him to elect us.'

before the foundation of the world, Cf 2 *Tim* 1.9. This proves that our election in Christ was no historical after-thought but the eternal resolve of unfettered sovereignty. 'Salvation is no precarious half-measure but a foundation laid in heaven' (E. K. Simpson). The acceptance of this truth leads to an unshakeable confidence in God even as it withers all confidence in the flesh [1 *Cor* 1.27–31].

that we should be holy and blameless before him.[1] (RSV) The ultimate purpose of our election in Christ was that we should be perfectly holy and without blame before him who is the searcher of every heart. Such spiritual perfection clearly pertains to the heavenly state, but because God's decree not only determines the *end* but also includes the *means* of attaining that end, he moves and enables the elect to persevere and pro-gress in holiness until what was begun in grace is at last con-summated in glory [cf *Phil* 2.12, 13; 2 *Thess* 2.13]. From this it follows, 'First, that individuals, and not communities or nations, are the objects of election; secondly, that holiness in no form can be the ground of election. If men are chosen to be holy, they cannot be chosen because they are holy. And, thirdly, it follows that holiness is the only evidence of election. For one who lives in sin to claim to be elected unto holiness, is a contradiction' (Charles Hodge) [2 *Pet* 1.3–11].

*V*5: **having foreordained us unto adoption as sons through Jesus Christ unto himself, according to the good pleasure of his will,**

1. As the emphasis throughout this passage is upon the spontaneous love of the Father, it is more appropriate to link 'in love' with the act of foreordaining his people to sonship [*v* 5] than to read 'blameless before him in love' [*v* 4], which less fittingly attributes the primary reference to love in the Epistle to our secondary response.

having in love foreordained us unto adoption as sons through Jesus Christ (ASV margin). Clearly this is no coldly conceived decree, for nothing but predestinating *love* can account for our adoption into the family of God as his sons! This elevation of us by grace to the status and privileges of sonship could be effected only through the redemptive mediation of the One who is the Father's Son by nature [*Rom* 8.29]. The experience of this filial relationship is a present reality in the life of believers [*Rom* 8.15; *Gal* 4.5], though its unveiling in glory remains as the hope of the future [*Rom* 8.23; 1 *John* 3.1–3].

unto himself, The phrase discloses the *goal* of God's foreordination of us to the standing of sons. It is to bring us 'to himself, into perfect fellowship with him, into adoring, loving relation to himself as the true end and object of our being' (Salmond).

according to the good pleasure of his will, These words signify something more than the determination of bare sovereignty, for the reference to God's 'good pleasure' brings out the fact that his gracious resolve to save the elect was wholly grounded in the free delight with which he *fore-loved* them [*Rom* 8.29].

*V*6: **to the praise of the glory of his grace, which he freely bestowed on us in the Beloved:**

to the praise of the glory of his grace, The heaping up of such genitival phrases is a striking feature of this letter, in which Paul so often struggles against the limitations of language as he endeavours to express the unutterable riches of God's grace. 'To' here shows that the glory of God is the great end in our election, and this consists in our ever increasing recognition ('the praise') of the manifested excellence ('of the glory') of God's undeserved bounty towards us ('of his grace').

which he freely bestowed on us in the Beloved: Paul again prompts our praise of God's unmerited favour by making a play on the word grace, for 'freely bestowed' really means 'be-graced' (Bruce). Thus he speaks of the 'grace' [*v* 6a] with which God 'be-graced' us in the Beloved. All the grace of God is lavished upon us in the supreme gift of his Son [*Rom* 8.32]. We are beloved of God only in the Beloved, in whom he is well pleased [*Matt* 3.17; 17.5; cf *Col* 1.13: 'the Son of his love']. As the title 'Saviour' regards our Lord from the point of view of men, so 'the Beloved' tells us what he is 'from the point of view of God – He is God's unique One, the object of his supreme choice, who stands related to him in the intimacy of appropriating love' (B. B. Warfield, *The Lord of Glory*, p. 246).

V7: **in whom we have our redemption through his blood, the forgiveness of our trespasses, according to the riches of his grace,**

The necessary consequence of God's eternal election is seen in Christ's saving work, for those who are chosen by the Father are the very ones who are redeemed by the Son [*vv* 7–12]. 'If, then, redemption be in order to accomplish the purpose of the sovereign election of some, then it is certain that Christ died in order to secure the salvation of the elect, and not in order to make the salvation of all men possible' (A. A. Hodge, *The Atonement*, p. 370).

in whom we have redemption through his blood, 'In whom' exclusively ascribes redemption to the unique achievement of God's beloved Son, in whom alone 'we have our redemption.' Modern attempts to reduce the meaning of this

[23]

word to the idea of mere deliverance are here ruled out by the qualifying phrase 'through his blood.' Those who limit 're-demption' to an act of emancipation empty the word of its saving content, for our release from the bondage of sin was a great *rescue by ransom* wrought out for us by the One who paid the price to set us free [cf *Mark* 10.45; *Rom* 3.24; *Heb* 9.12; 1 *Pet* 1.18, 19]. The 'final' redemption of 1.14 and 4.30 still rests upon this initial ransoming, the effects of which stretch into the future to secure our ultimate deliverance from the power and presence of evil in all its forms [*Luke* 21.28; *Rom* 8.23]. 'Through his blood' poignantly recalls the violent and shameful death that Christ willingly endured as the ap-pointed substitute of those who constitute the church, which he loved and came into the world to purchase at the cost of his all [5.25; *Acts* 20.28; 1 *Cor* 6.20].

the forgiveness of our trespasses, This linking of 'forgive-ness' with the death of Christ proves that the cancellation or remission of the penalty due to sin is based upon his payment of that debt on our behalf [*Matt* 26.28]. For 'sin is forgiven only as it is borne' (James Denney). The plural 'trespasses' draws attention to the many false steps, or deviations from God's standard of absolute righteousness, for which we daily stand in need of his forgiving grace. And this forgiveness, or sending away of our sins [*Ps* 103.12], we are said to *have* (present tense) in Christ. 'We are ever needing, and so are *ever having it,* for we are still "in him," and the merit of his blood is unexhausted. Forgiveness is not a blessing complete at any point of time in our human existence, and therefore we are still receiving it' (John Eadie) [1 *John* 1.7–9.]. The per-fection of God's provision in Christ shows the folly of those who seek the remission of sins by other methods of their own devising. Hence this inclusive faith demands the exclusive con-fession that 'there is none other name under heaven given among men, whereby we must be saved' [*Acts* 4.12].

according to the riches of his grace, This is the *measure* of God's limitless generosity towards us in Christ: it is '*according to* the riches of his grace.' 'Riches' is one of Paul's favourite words [*Rom* 2.4; 9.23; 11.12; 11.33; 2 *Cor* 8.2; *Phil* 4.19; *Col* 1.27], which is also much in evidence in Ephesians [*v* 18; 2.7; 3.8, 16]. He uses it here to underscore the fact that God's securement of our free forgiveness was a costly matter. As Thomas Goodwin says, 'Thou needest not bring one penny. God is rich enough.' It is well that it is so, for how can beggars bring anything towards the forgiveness of their sins? Nothing but the overwhelming munificence of God's grace can suffice for that!

*V*8: **which he made to abound toward us in all wisdom and prudence;**

The profusion of God's grace in Christ is next stated to be received by us in the form of 'all wisdom and prudence.' It is because Christ 'was made unto us wisdom' [1 *Cor* 1.30] that we have the spiritual understanding to discern and appropriate the divine realities which remain hidden from the unbelieving [*v* 19], and the prudence or practical intelligence to apply that wisdom to all the varying situations of our life. 'Wisdom is the knowledge which sees into the heart of things, which knows them as they really are. Prudence is the understanding which leads to right action' (J. Armitage Robinson).

*V*9: **making known unto us the mystery of his will, according to his good pleasure which he purposed in him**

This overflowing of God's grace towards us 'in all wisdom and prudence' took effect in the disclosure of 'the mystery of his will.' In the New Testament a 'mystery' is not an unexplained riddle, but a divine secret which, though proclaimed to all, is understood only by those whom the Spirit of God enlightens [*Mark* 4.11; 1 *Cor* 2.7–16]. Thus God's plan of salvation, once the secret of his unfathomable will, is now being revealed to all included within its scope. For it is through the worldwide preaching of the gospel that this mystery is made known to the elect who are *given* ears to hear and hearts to receive it [cf *Acts* 13.48; 16.14; 18.9, 10]. But there is one aspect of that plan which engages the particular attention of the apostle in Ephesians and Colossians, namely, the amazing inclusion of Gentiles as well as Jews within the same household of faith [2.11–22; 3.3–9; *Col* 1.26, 27].

The manifestation of the mystery was 'according to his good pleasure.' It was God's special delight to reveal the secret of his love to the sons of men, and as Paul never tires of pointing out, it was a love which embraced them in the Beloved. Hence he adds, 'which he purposed *in him*.' The Father's purpose was *in the Son*, 'inasmuch as it was to take effect through the Son, incarnate, sacrificed, and glorified; and further, as it concerned a church which was to be incorporated "into Christ" ' (H. C. G. Moule) [*Rom* 8.28, 29].

*V*10: **unto a dispensation of the fulness of the times, to sum up all things in Christ, the things in the heavens, and the things upon the earth; in him,** *I say*,

with a view to a dispensation belonging to the fulness of the times,

'Dispensation' (*oikonomia*) is a word that primarily refers to house-management, and the meaning here is that God has entrusted Christ with the 'administration' of that purpose which is the good pleasure of his will [*v* 9]. Just as a great landowner appoints a manager to put into execution his plans for the estate, so the Father has given Christ full authority to administer and bring to completion the entire plan of salvation [*Matt*

28.18]. 'The fulness of the times' points forward to this epoch of consummation, whereas in *Gal* 4.4 'the fulness of the time' covers the more restricted period of Christ's first advent.

(namely) to sum up under one head all things in Christ, the things in the heavens, and the things upon the earth;

Paul now explains that the object which God had in view was the summing up of all things in Christ. This is one of several verses in Ephesians and Colossians in which the apostle sets forth the cosmic significance of Christ's person and work [*vv* 20-22; *Col.* 1.15-20]. No doubt this teaching was directed against the heretical speculations of those 'gnostics' whose superior 'knowledge' had relegated Christ to an inferior rôle through the unlawful exaltation of a host of angelic intermediaries. Although opinion is divided over the precise meaning of 'to sum up' [*anakephalaioō*: used only here and in *Rom* 13.9], the rendering 'to sum up under one head' is not unlikely in a passage that goes on to speak of Christ as the Head of the church [*v* 22]. It would seem that Paul has two headships in mind: Christ's sovereign headship of the cosmos, and his redemptive headship of the church [*Acts* 20. 28]. When it is recognized that the church does not include 'all things,' the danger of confusing the saving effects of Christ's work with its cosmic consequences is avoided. The passage does not teach the universal salvation of all men; it states that God will sum up the whole creation under Christ through whom 'all things' shall find their true coherence and unity [cf *Rom* 8.19-23]. Thus the apostle's reference is to 'the entire harmony of the universe, which shall no longer contain alien and discordant elements, but of which all the parts shall find their centre and bond of union in Christ. Sin and death, sorrow and failure and suffering, shall cease. There shall be a new heaven and a new earth' (J. B. Lightfoot).

[27]

in him, *I say*, This is to be connected with the following verse.

*V*11: **in whom also we were made a heritage, having been foreordained according to the purpose of him who worketh all things after the counsel of his will;**

It was in fulfilment of God's eternal design that in Christ 'we' – i.e. *all* believers as represented by Paul and his readers – were actually 'made a heritage,' or taken for God's inheritance. This rendering is preferable to that of the AV, 'in whom also we have obtained an inheritance,' because it is more consistent with the context which speaks of 'God's own possession' [*v* 14] and 'his inheritance in the saints' [*v* 18]. The apostle's appropriation of this Old Testament title for Christian use indicates the spiritual fulfilment in the church [*Gal* 6.16] of that election which had singled out national Israel as God's peculiar possession [cf *Deut* 4.20; 9.29; 32.9]. 'That God should be his people's portion is easy to be accounted for, for he is their joy and felicity; but how they should be his portion, who neither needs them, nor can be benefited by them, must be resolved into the wondrous condescensions of free grace. *Even so, Father, because it seemed good in thine eyes* so to call them and count them' (Matthew Henry on *Deut* 32.9).

Since believers may never ascribe their privileged position to the power of their own choice [*John* 1.13], Paul again states that God's foreordination was the cause of this saving change [*v* 5]. Thus the calling out to faith in Christ of God's heritage (which consists of those elect Jews and Gentiles who together make up the universal church) takes place 'according to the purpose of him who worketh all things after the counsel of his will.' In God's execution of his great plan of salvation nothing is left to 'chance,' and nothing is contingent upon the will of the creature, because nothing is exempted from his sovereign control. For God 'works' (his energy is dynamically operative in) 'all things,' not arbitrarily but intelligently, in order to fulfil what he had determined to accomplish in the eternal 'counsel' of his grace [Rom 8.28].

V12: **to the end that we should be unto the praise of his glory, we who had before hoped in Christ:**

to the end that we should be to the praise of his glory, we who beforehand had centred our hope in Christ (Hendriksen). It is more in keeping with the inclusive scope of the passage to regard the verse as giving expression to the common Christian hope in Christ's return than to restrict 'we' to the priority of the Jewish hope in the Messiah. Those who do so are bound to maintain that the 'you' of the following verse refers to Gentile believers, but such a division would limit 'the praise of his glory' to Jews and apportion 'the Holy Spirit of promise' to Gentiles! It is therefore preferable to accept the interpretation offered in Moule's paraphrase: 'That we should contribute to the glory of God, at the appearing of Christ; welcomed then as the once patient and expectant believers in his promise while still it tarried' [Rom 8.24, 25].

V13: **in whom ye also, having heard the word of the truth, the gospel of your salvation, – in whom, having also believed, ye were sealed with the Holy Spirit of promise;**

Paul's majestic opening sentence approaches its climax with the change of address which thankfully recalls his readers' participation in the gift of the Holy Spirit through the gracious act of God [vv 13, 14]. The main thought of the verse is: **in whom** (in Christ) **ye** (Ephesians) **also** (in common with all other Christians) **. . . were sealed.** The connection is difficult because the construction is broken by the apostle's characteristic insistence upon the necessity of faith. And his

teaching is that the believing and the sealing always go together. As there is no sealing without believing, so there is
no believing without sealing. Hence this is not an experience
reserved for a favoured few; *it is the birthright of all believers*!

**having heard the word of the truth, the gospel of your
salvation,** – But as no one can believe in him of whom he
has never heard, Paul first refers to the preaching through
which the Ephesians had been brought to faith in Christ [*Rom*
10.14–17]. Objectively, this message is 'the word' that has the
truth for its essential content [*Col* 1.5]; and subjectively, it
became 'the gospel' or good news of *their* salvation when they
believed it for themselves [*Rom* 1.16].

**in whom, having also believed, ye were sealed with the
Holy Spirit of promise,** 'Having believed' is the coincident
aorist participle and Paul's use of it here shows that they were
not sealed *after*, but *when* they believed (exactly as in *Acts* 19.2:
'Did ye receive the Holy Spirit *when ye believed*?'). This distinction is important because it means that the two verbs
must be seen as the two sides of the same event: in the moment
when they believed, they were also sealed. Hence the sealing
is not represented as a process, but as a definite act which was
at once complete. Moreover, the further use of 'in whom'
indicates the impossibility of separating the experience of
being 'in Christ' from the sealing which is common to all believers [cf the universal language of 2 *Cor* 1.21, 22].

It is not necessary to read any reference to baptism into the
text to explain what this sealing means. In the ancient world
visible seals were used to attest as genuine, to mark ownership,
and to keep secure. But as this seal cannot be seen, its presence
may be known only by its characteristic effects [*John* 3.8]. So
believers are authenticated as the children of God by the inward witness of the Spirit [*Rom* 8.16]. And it is because they
are sealed by a living Person who can be grieved by sin, that

they may lose for a time this subjective assurance of their salvation, even though they remain objectively sealed unto the day of redemption [4.30]. Consequently, the adjective 'holy,' placed emphatically at the end of the clause, points to the kind of separation which is always demanded by him, whose essential attribute is holiness [cf *Rom* 8.1–14]. He is also the 'promised' Spirit, whose advent ushered in the long-awaited era of gospel grace. 'It is clear that what is in view here is not the extraordinary or miraculous gifts of the Spirit, but that bestowal of the Spirit in which all believers shared, which was the subject of the great Old Testament prophecies [*Joel* 2.28–32; *Is* 32.15; 44.3; *Ezek* 36.26; 39,29; *Zech* 12.10], and of which a new heart, a new spirit, was to be the result' (Salmond).

*V*14: **which is an earnest of our inheritance, unto the redemption of *God's* own possession, unto the praise of his glory.**

Paul enlarges on the theme of the believer's assurance of final salvation, already implied in the concept of sealing, by stating that the Holy Spirit is also 'an earnest' of our inheritance. This is the deposit that is given as the guarantee that the full amount will be paid later. It is not simply a pledge, which might be different in kind, but the first instalment. 'In other words the thing given is related to the thing assured – the present to the hereafter – as a part to the whole. It is the same in kind' (Lightfoot). So the gift of the Holy Spirit is the beginning of salvation, the first instalment of the Christian's future inheritance. The same truth is expressed under a different metaphor in *Rom* 8.23, where the Spirit is compared to 'the first-fruits' of the final harvest. As Lightfoot further observes, 'The actual spiritual life of the Christian is the same in kind as his future glorified life; the kingdom of heaven is a present kingdom; the believer is already seated on the right hand of God . . . Nevertheless the present gift of the Spirit is only a *small fraction* of the future endowment. This idea also would be suggested by the usual relation between the earnest-money and the full payment.' Thus we must recognize in the gift of the Spirit the indisputable proof of God's determination to honour all the obligations he has assumed towards us under the covenant of grace [*Phil* 1.6]. Yet it would be a grave mistake to conceive of this gift in any static sense, for our present realization of future glory admits of spiritual increase *in this world* [cf comment on *v* 17 and 3.16].

unto the redemption of *God's* own possession, This looks forward to the day of ultimate deliverance when God shall finally claim us as his special possession [*Mal* 3.17; 1 *Pet* 2.9]. Paul's language in this passage clearly shows that he is thinking of the church as the new Israel, for he applies to Gentiles the very terms – 'promise,' 'inheritance,' 'possession' – which were used to describe Israel's peculiar privileges. Now it is by *our* possession of the Spirit that we are already marked out as *God's* own possession. And this means that it is only by receiving the Spirit, who is the very essence of the new covenant [*Gal* 3.14], that a man is made a member of the new Israel and participates in the blessings of the new age.

unto the praise of his glory. We must never confuse God's glory with the vain egoism of man's boasting. For since *God is God* he could set no higher object before himself than the complete manifestation of his own glory. Thus the fulfilment of his purpose of grace in the salvation of the elect shall eternally redound to the praise of his glory, which is the great end of all creation [*Rev* 4.11].

*V*15: **For this cause I also, having heard of the faith in the Lord Jesus which is among you, and the love which *ye show* toward all the saints;**

Filled with thanksgiving by the knowledge that the Ephesians share in the blessings just enumerated [*vv* 3–14], and having heard of their continued progress since he last saw them, Paul now begins his great prayer for their further enlightenment [*vv* 15–23]. Those who deny Paul's authorship of the Epistle regard 'having heard' as a proof of their argument that the writer was not personally acquainted with his readers [as in *Col* 1.4]. But this assumes too much, for the same language is used in *Philem* 4, 5 and Paul certainly knew Philemon! 'May one not *hear* of friends from whom one has been absent for five years?' (Lenski). Obviously, one may hear about persons whom one has met (the Ephesians, Philemon) as well as about persons whom one has never met (the Colossians). Note that the Ephesians showed the reality of their 'faith' in the Lord Jesus by the sincerity of their 'love' toward all the saints. 'Faith is but an empty name if it does not fructify in love. Faith in Christ is only a delusion if it issues not in love for those who are his' (Arthur W. Pink) [1 *John* 3.14; 4.20, 21].

*V*16: **cease not to give thanks for you, making mention** *of you* **in my prayers;**

It is very striking that Paul never congratulates his readers on their faith, but always thanks God for it.[1] And this is because

1. A fact which is entirely in harmony with the teaching of the opening doxology. Cf *The Westminster Confession of Faith*, Ch. 10, sections I and II: 'All those whom God hath predestinated unto life, and those only, he is pleased, in his appointed and accepted time, effectually to call, by his Word and Spirit, out of that state of sin and death in which they are by nature, to grace and salvation by Jesus Christ; enlightening their minds spiritually and savingly to understand the things of God; taking away their heart of stone, and giving unto them an heart of flesh; renewing their wills, and by his almighty power determining them to that which is good; and effectually drawing them to Jesus Christ; yet so as they come most freely, being made willing by his grace.

'This effectual call is of God's free and special grace alone, not from every genuine conversion is a signal instance of the putting forth of God's almighty power [cf *vv* 19, 20 with 2.1, 5]. But Paul not only regarded the Ephesian Christians as a constant cause for thankfulness to God, he also saw them as standing in need of his continual prayers on their behalf. 'How much of the Apostle's work for his converts consisted in the holy labour of special intercessory prayer, with thanksgiving! In his Roman lodging this was the case, perhaps, even more than ever' (Moule).

V17: that the God of our Lord Jesus Christ, the Father of glory, may give unto you a spirit of wisdom and revelation in the knowledge of him;

Paul here prays that God, who is the fountain of all grace and the Father of glory, may give his readers the wisdom and revelation of the Spirit which will increase their knowledge of him (i.e. God). It is as the God of our Mediator, the Lord Jesus Christ, that God is seen to be the sole source of grace for sinful men [cf 1.3]. Moreover, there is an intermingling of grace in the sublime title, Father of glory; for God is not only the One to whom all glory belongs, but also the bestower of the glory by which his children are enlightened and transformed [*Ps* 84.11; 2 *Cor* 3.18; 4.6].

The fact that 'Spirit' lacks the article is no reason to exclude a personal reference to the Holy Spirit, for only he can impart wisdom and revelation to men. The apostle's request is that believers may have more of the Spirit as the Spirit of wisdom, so that they may have an enlarged understanding of that wis-

---

any thing at all foreseen in man; who is altogether passive therein, until, being quickened and renewed by the Holy Spirit, he is thereby enabled to answer this call, and to embrace the grace offered and conveyed in it.'

dom which must be not only preached *to us* but also revealed
in us [1 *Cor* 2.10ff.]. For we are blind and understand 'nothing
of God's spiritual grace, unless he opens our eyes and takes
away the veil that is upon them, and even gives us a new
sight which we do not have. For our eyes are worse than put
out until he enlightens them by his Holy Spirit' (Calvin).

And it is through this endowment that they will acquire a
greater knowledge of God. As J. Armitage Robinson rightly
points out, this is not abstract knowledge, but 'knowledge
directed towards a particular object' in the sense of perceiving,
discerning, and recognizing God as 'the God of our Lord
Jesus Christ, the Father of glory.' It is therefore a warm personal knowledge of God as he is revealed in Christ [*John* 14.6].
Philosophy comes to us with the man-centred message, 'Know
thyself'; whereas the *summun bonum* of the inspired Word is,
'Know thy God'.

*V*18: **having the eyes of your heart enlightened, that ye
may know what is the hope of his calling, what the
riches of the glory of his inheritance in the saints,**
*V*19: **and what the exceeding greatness of his power to
us-ward who believe, according to that working of the
strength of his might,**

In Scripture 'the heart' denotes what a man is in his deepest
self; it is the seat of his intellectual, religious, and moral life.
It is because man is inwardly blinded by sin that the light
which is within him is darkness until the Spirit shines into his
heart in re-creating grace [*Matt* 6.23; 2 *Cor* 4.6]. But as this
initial illumination is only the beginning of what must be a
continuous process, Paul prays that the Ephesians may enjoy
such further enlightenment of the inner vision as will enable
them to grasp the three great realities of their faith.

[35]

that ye may know what is the hope of his calling, 1. It is the eternal choice of God that makes this an *effectual* calling and a *certain* hope. Hence it is with no fragile confidence in their own resources that believers are to face the future, but with the assured hope that the God, who called them to eternal life in Christ by giving them the earnest of the Spirit [*v* 14], will soon invest them with the promised glory [*Rom* 15.13].

what the riches of the glory of his inheritance in the saints, 2. Although God's people are called to a glorious inheritance, Paul here returns to the amazing thought that they are also an inheritance for God [*vv* 11, 14]. They are 'his own possession, in whom he will display to the universe the untold riches of his glory. We can scarcely realize what it must mean to God to see his purpose complete, to see creatures of his hand, sinners redeemed by his grace, reflecting his own glory' (F. F. Bruce).

and what the exceeding greatness of his power to usward who believe, according to that working of the strength of his might, 3. The Ephesians must not only have in view God's past calling and God's future inheritance, but also realize God's power in their present experience; for the continued progress of believers in the way that leads to glory entirely depends upon the exceeding greatness of that *power*, whose measure is further defined by an awkward but impressive accumulation of synonyms. According to T. K. Abbott, this *working* or actual exercise of the *strength* of God's inherent power is that *might* which overcomes all resistance. Thus Paul's request is that believers may recognize that the power which awakened them from the sleep of death will invincibly bring them to heaven, for it is the same power which raised Christ from the dead [*v* 20].

*V*20: **which he wrought in Christ, when he raised him from the dead, and made him to sit at his right hand in the heavenly** *places*;

As the Word made flesh Jesus can speak of raising himself by his own power [*John* 2.19, 21; 10.17, 18], but Paul always refers the resurrection of our Head to the direct act of God because this set the seal of divine approval upon Christ's work for us [cf *Rom* 4.24, 25; 8.34]. Without this act of omnipotent power the apostles would have had no gospel to preach [1 *Cor* 15.14, 15]. 'Had he not emerged from the tomb, all our hopes, all our salvation would be lying dead with him unto this day ... The resurrection of Christ is thus the indispensable evidence of his completed work, his accomplished redemption' (B. B. Warfield: 'The Resurrection of Christ a Fundamental Doctrine,' *Selected Shorter Writings*, Vol. 1, p. 200). And it is because believers already know the power of Christ's resurrection that they enjoy the consequent assurance of participating in the resurrection of the just [*Rom* 8.11, 23].

An equally important place is given to the exaltation of Christ by the New Testament writers who see it as the fulfilment of what was foretold in *Ps* 110.1 [cf *Acts* 5.31; 7.56; *Rom* 8.34; 1 *Cor* 15.25; *Phil* 2.9–11; *Col* 3.1; *Heb* 1.3; 8.1; 12.2; *Rev* 5.1–14]. This sharing of God's throne at once demonstrates the divine dignity of Christ and proclaims his universal lordship [*Heb* 1.13; 1 *Pet* 3.22]. He is represented as seated, not to denote his permanent posture in heaven [*Acts* 7.56; *Rev* 2.1], but to show that he has finished the work of redemption and entered upon the exercise of that power which belongs to his heavenly state [*Acts* 3.21]. And though Christ's people are to see in his glorification the pledge of their future glory, Paul's special concern in Ephesians is not with the ultimate but the *present* consequences of this enthronement for believers [1.3, 2.6; cf *Col* 3.1ff.].

*V*21: **far above all rule, and authority, and power, and dominion, and every name that is named, not only in this world, but also in that which is to come:**
*V*22a: **and he put all things in subjection under his feet,**

Paul affirms Christ's lordship over all created powers, probably with a sidelong glance at the false teaching in Asia Minor that denied the finality of Christ's mediation by paying homage to angels [*Col* 2.18]. In comparing this enumeration of angelic orders with that given in *Col* 1.16, Lightfoot insists that no stress can be laid on the sequence of names, as though Paul were formulating a precise doctrine of the celestial hierarchy. He clearly has no patience with this elaborate angelology, and brushes aside these speculations without remarking upon how much or how little truth there may be in them. For the one fact which every believer must hold fast is that the exalted Christ is far above 'every name that is named' [*Phil* 2.9]. 'The decisive point for Paul is that in no regard, whether as fate, or nature, or intermediate beings, or servants of God, can these powers either separate the Christian from Christ or lead him to Him' (W. Foerster, *TDNT*, Vol. II, p. 573).

Furthermore, this supremacy belongs to Christ 'not only in this age, but also in that which is to come.' Paul's adoption of the Jewish concept of the two ages was modified by his teaching that in the experience of believers the future had already invaded the present age [1.3, 2.6; *Phil* 3.20]. This was made visually plain by Geerhardus Vos[1] in two diagrams:

I. THE ORIGINAL SCHEME

| This age or world | The age or world to come |

---

1. *The Pauline Eschatology*, p. 38.

II. THE MODIFIED SCHEME

The world to come,
realized in principle

Resurrection of Christ	(in Heaven) (on earth)	Parousia	Future age and world realized in solid existence

This age or world

Hence it is the function of faith to acknowledge the reality of Christ's rule during the very period when all the unbelieving are blind to it – a lesson which is enforced by Paul's quotation of *Ps* 8.6 [cf *Heb* 2.6ff].

and he put all things in subjection under his feet, After Christ's triumph over principalities and powers on the cross [*Col* 2.15], God exalted him to the throne of the universe and put all things under his feet. Despite present appearances to the contrary, the victory of the cross has secured the final doom of Satan and his hosts, though in the meanwhile believers must contest his usurped power well knowing that the ultimate issue of this spiritual warfare is not in doubt [6.11, 12; *Rom* 16.20; 1 *Cor* 15.25]. Paul here shows that David's words find their proper fulfilment in the Son of Man whose conquest of sin and death has invested him with a domination far more glorious than that which was lost to the race through Adam's fall.

*V*22b: **and gave him to be head over all things to the church,**
*V*23: **which is his body, the fulness of him that filleth all in all.**

Paul further states that this universal lordship is exercised for the benefit of the church: God gave *him* – who is over all things – to be Head 'to' (or rather 'for') the church. 'Christ therefore has power over all things in heaven and on earth, and in a specific sense he is the King over his church, which he rules by his grace and Spirit and Word. The relation between this power over all things and his sovereignty over his church is such, that he employs the former to the preservation and salvation of the latter' (Herman Hoeksema, *Reformed Dogmatics*, p. 627). This headship of Christ means: 1. He is the sole ruler of the church [5.23ff], so that it must refuse submission to the alien yoke of state or pope; 2. He is the sole source of its life and strength, so that it receives from him that nourishment which promotes the growth of the whole body [4.15, 16].

which is his body, The final development of this familiar Pauline metaphor is reached in Colossians and Ephesians. When the church is compared to the body of Christ in the earlier Epistles it is the crucified body of Christ that is in view [1 *Cor* 10.16f; 11.23–27], whereas here the emphasis is upon the risen and glorified body [though the cross is not forgotten, cf 2.13ff; *Col* 2.14, 15]. What immediately follows shows that Paul is not speaking of the *outward witness* of the church, but of its *inward union* with Christ its Head. In Ephesians the main stress is placed on what the church receives from Christ and on its internal growth. This is certainly the prerequisite for its active service, but a different image is used to express that thought [cf 6.10–20].

the fulness of him that filleth all in all. A profound phrase whose meaning is the subject of much dispute. Some say that the church fills up that which is lacking in Christ who would be in some sense incomplete without his body; while others maintain that it is Christ who fills the church. The idea that the church is the complement of Christ is not favoured by the context, which is concerned with what Christ is to the church and not what the Church is to Christ. 'All that Christ has from God, the power, the gifts, the grace, he passes on to the church ... The church has nothing to give Christ of herself, by which what is lacking in him could be filled up. Instead, it is the church that is filled with him [cf 3.19], becoming a partaker of all that he owns and is, for the purpose of continuing his work' (Stig Hanson, *The Unity of the Church in the New Testament*, pp. 128–129).

CHAPTER TWO

Paul next reminds his readers of how they had been delivered by the grace of God from the deadness of their former walk in trespasses and sins, and quickened into a new life in Christ so that they are now able to walk in those good works which God had prepared for their doing [vv 1–10]. The apostle then goes on to show that this individual experience of salvation has the most far reaching corporate consequences. As Gentiles they were formerly aliens from the commonwealth of Israel, but now in Christ they are fellow-citizens with believing Jews and full members of the household of God. This spiritual unity was achieved by Christ's reconciling death which abolished the dividing wall that stood between them and created one new man, so that Jews and Gentiles are knit together into a holy temple in the Lord [vv 11–22].

V1: **And you** *did he make alive*, **when ye were dead through your trespasses and sins,**

The chapter begins with one grand sentence, which celebrates the greatness of the grace that raised the readers from the sepulchre of their sins [vv 1–10].

And you *did he make alive*, An emphatic address which says in effect: '*You* were the unworthy objects of distinguishing mercy!' But as Paul actually makes no reference to God's quickening grace until he has first made clear their abject plight by nature [*vv* 1–3], it is better to omit the italicized words supplied by the translators to ensure a smoother reading. It is vital to grasp the significance of the apostle's method [cf *Rom* ch. 1–3], because an inadequate doctrine of sin always leads to slight views of grace and also leaves ajar the door that admits error. ' "Never was there a heresy, but it had something to do with an insufficient estimate of sin." And an insufficient estimate of the "thing which God hateth" is not only the parent of speculative error; it is the secret death of true spiritual joy' (Moule, *Ephesian Studies*, p. 70).

when ye were dead through your trespasses and sins,
'Trespasses and sins' are two plurals which vividly recall the multiplied aggravation of their guilt before God.[1] Being dead while they lived, their activity was then the activity of death [*vv* 2,3]. This deadness made them insensible of their separation from the life of God [4.18] and of his just condemnation of their wayward walk [*v* 3], even as it also left them without either the ability or the inclination to arise from the tomb [*v* 5]. Thus they were destitute of all *spiritual* life, 'having no hope,' because they were 'without God in the world' [*vv* 11, 12].

*V*2: **wherein ye once walked according to the course of this world, according to the prince of the powers of the air, of the spirit that now worketh in the sons of disobedience;**

Paul uses the verb 'to walk' as a graphic metaphor to denote deliberate progress in a particular direction. Here it points to the voluntary adoption of a life-style which was utterly op-

---

1. But if the terms are not used synonymously, then 'trespasses' would indicate the deliberate transgression of the law, while 'sins' would point to the 'missing of the mark' set for them by God.

posed to the standard set for man by God [cf 4.17–19]. Hence the spiritually *dead* are in a state of *active* opposition to God, for which they are justly held responsible.

according to the course of this world, The former conduct of the readers was in complete conformity to the transient norm of worldly life, and was a total contradiction of the spiritual norm of the kingdom of God. So that while they embraced the corrupt and debased standard of 'this present evil world' [*Gal* 1.4], they walked in nothing but trespasses and sins.

according to the ruler of the kingdom of the air (Arndt-Gingrich). Although they had chosen to live in this way, and were certainly accountable for their actions, they could not have chosen otherwise. For at that time they were under Satan's sway, and served him as the willing captives of his realm [*Col* 1.13; *2 Tim* 2.26]. Some say that 'air' should be understood figuratively, but William Hendriksen presents a convincing argument for its literal meaning. He concludes: 'This passage, in conjunction with others [3.10, 15; 6.12], clearly teaches that God has tenanted the supermundane realm with innumerable hosts, and that in its lower region the minions of Satan are engaged in their destructive missions'.

of the spirit that now worketh in the sons of disobedience;

According to F. F. Bruce, this means that Satan is the governing power behind the 'spirit of the age' [cf 1 *John* 5.19], which is so powerfully at work in 'the sons of disobedience.' As this Hebraism indicates, the disobedience is not incidental but innate. It describes those whose lives are wholly characterized by disobedience. Paul's reference to the *present* activity of this spirit in the unregenerate serves to remind believers of their gracious deliverance from its enslaving power.

*V*3 : **among whom we also all once lived in the lusts of our flesh, doing the desires of the flesh and of the mind, and were by nature children of wrath, even as the rest:-**

Among these we all once lived in the passions of our flesh, (RSV). It was among these sons of disobedience that 'we all' – Paul as well as the Ephesians – who now believe, once lived in the same bondage to the imperious dictates of our 'flesh'. Here the word has its full ethical meaning, *viz.* fallen human nature as alienated from God and under the dominion of sin. 'At one time "our flesh" governed us completely. It is its nature to produce nothing but sinful desires and appetites that call for sinful satisfaction' (Lenski).

following the desires of body and mind, (RSV). As the RSV correctly indicates, 'flesh' now receives the more restricted meaning of 'body' from its juxtaposition with 'mind'. Thus the lusts of the flesh are not limited to the sins of the *body*, but also include the sins of the *mind*. 'Both are under the same dominion of sin, and together constitute that natural life in the flesh which is enmity against God' (John Macpherson). [*Rom* 8.7, 8].

and we were, in our natural condition (as descendants of Adam), **children of wrath** (Arndt-Gingrich). This reveals the spring of our corruption. For what man *does* can only be explained by what man *is*; his personal transgressions are the result of inborn depravity. So through Adam's one act of disobedience [*Rom* 5.12ff] we are born 'children of wrath' – another Hebraism which shows that we deserve nothing but wrath. And since nothing evokes God's wrath but sin, it is evident that *original sin* must be something more than a mere theological figment!

like the rest of mankind. (RSV). At one time we believers were just like all the rest! The ultimate reason for this contrast is that God has chosen us in love [1.4, 5], and has thus made us to differ from 'the rest', who by nature were the same as ourselves. Up to the time of our conversion there was no difference. The contrast therefore is between nature and grace.

V4: **but God, being rich in mercy, for his great love wherewith he loved us,**

'But God' points to the Author of this transition from wrath to grace. It was not simply the misery of our plight which called forth God's mercy, for he left multitudes to perish in their sin [*Rom* 9.15, 16]. No, the reason we received these riches of mercy was because of the greatness of that love which he bore towards us 'in Christ'. And as God never acts ineffectively, it is a degradation of the gospel to depict him as *helplessly* pleading with men to respond to his love! For at the very outset of this letter Paul makes it crystal clear that God's love always reaches its intended objects [1.3–14]. 'Us' here means 'we who now believe', it is through faith that we are brought to realize our interest in the eternal covenant of grace. Until we believe there is nothing to distinguish us from other men, for we are 'by nature children of wrath, even as the rest'. Scholars have commented upon the confessional character of this passage [*vv* 1–10], but we must recognize that the ability to make such a statement of faith is the result of God's quickening grace [*v* 5]. Scripture does not present us with a God whose hands are tied until man chooses to believe the gospel; it declares that God will assuredly call the elect to saving faith through the preaching of the gospel to every creature [*Is* 55.11; *Acts* 13.48].

V5: **even when we were dead through our trespasses, made us alive together with Christ (by grace have ye been saved),**

even when we were dead through our trespasses, Paul is about to introduce the verb which (in the Greek) has been held back from ver. 1, but before doing so he introduces another modifier to heighten the contrast between our former deadness and the power of God's grace. For it is marvellous that God should quicken dead men who are worthy of nothing but everlasting damnation. As John Trapp says, Paul repeats himself because we find his doctrine so difficult to believe. We are apt to think 'better of ourselves than there is cause for, and can hardly be persuaded that we are dead in sins and trespasses, and lie rotting and stinking in the graves of corruption, much worse than Lazarus did after he had lain four days in his sepulchre.'

(God) . . . made us alive together with Christ At last we are given the *compound* verb which shows that God's act of quickening united us *with* Christ [cf *v* 6: 'raised up *with*' and 'made to sit *with*']. These remarkable verses set forth our present participation in Christ's heavenly life more clearly than any other passage in the New Testament. As the article in the original indicates ('the Christ'), Christ is here considered in his official relation to us. Accordingly his resurrection is seen as the pledge and pattern of our spiritual quickening. When he was physically raised, all his people were *ideally* raised in him; and because of this prior union with him, they are, in regeneration, *actually* quickened and raised with him (Eadie).

(by grace have ye been saved), Paul's characteristic parenthesis further emphasizes the grace by which our salvation has been secured. 'Nothing else than grace could give life to the dead, but grace could indeed do even that' (Salmond). Here it is important to note the force of the perfect tense, which points to a present state as the continuing result of a past action. Salvation is complete with respect to our deliverance from the death of sin, but incomplete with respect to what is still reserved for us [*Rom* 8.24].

*V*6: **and raised us up with him, and made us to sit with him in the heavenly** *places*, **in Christ Jesus:**

It is because Christ is our Head, both in the judicial and organic sense of the word, that he did not ascend to heaven in any private capacity, but as representing all the elect. As the Head of his own, he bore all our iniquities and obtained eternal righteousness. His righteousness is our righteousness; his death is our death; his resurrection is our resurrection. And so in that legal sense his ascension is our ascension. We sit with him in heavenly places. But he is also our Head in an organic sense, As we are his members we can never be separated from him. Hence he could not return to heaven without taking us with him. And because we are already *spiritually* present with him, we know that he will soon draw us to himself [1 *John* 3.2]. Thus all who are regenerated by the Spirit partake of the heavenly life of their Lord, so that they now fix their affections on things above [*Col* 3.1–4].[1] 'Your head is in heaven; if your heart be there too, you are members of his mystical body . . . Christ may lose members [hypocrites], as he is head of a visible church, but not as he is head of a mystical body' (Thomas Manton, *Exposition of John XVII*, pp. 168, 226).

in Christ Jesus: [cf 1.13]. The concluding phrase qualifies the whole statement. 'This quickening, this resurrection, this seating of us with him take effect in so far as we are *in* him as our Representative, having our life and our completeness in our Head' (Salmond).

*V*7: **that in the ages to come he might show the exceeding riches of his grace in kindness toward us in Christ Jesus:**

1. Condensed from Herman Hoeksema's *Reformed Dogmatics*, pp. 425–6, and *The Triple Knowledge*, Vol. II, pp. 74–76.

This verse shows us that the manifestation of God's glory is the chief end of our salvation. 'The purpose of God for his church, as Paul came to understand it, reaches beyond itself, beyond the salvation, the enlightenment and the re-creation of individuals, beyond its unity and fellowship, beyond even its witness to the world. The church is to be the exhibition to the whole creation of the wisdom and love and grace of God in Christ' (Francis Foulkes). Since 'the ages to come' is simply 'a plural of immensity' (Vos), the meaning is that only eternity will suffice for the complete display of the surpassing riches of God's grace in that kindness which he has shown us 'in Christ Jesus.' Here again the richness of the thought accounts for the apparent extravagance of the language. It is probable that in using the word 'kindness' Paul had in mind God's special act of kindness in giving Christ to be 'the saviour of the body' [2.13, 16; 5.23].

*V*8: **for by grace have ye been saved through faith; and that not of yourselves, *it is* the gift of God;**

'For it is by *this* grace that you have been saved.' With this re-assertion of what has already been parenthetically stated in ver. 5, Paul exultantly attributes the Ephesians' salvation to the solitary achievement of God's grace. 'Through faith' in no way detracts from the grace which bestows this priceless boon upon us, for the preposition used (*dia*) shows that faith was only the instrumental means of our receiving it. 'The hands of all other graces are working hands, but the hands of faith are merely receiving hands' (Goodwin).

and that not of yourselves, *it is* the gift of God; Ever jealous of God's glory, Paul adds that even this faith is not self-generated; it is the gift of God! When we are thus dependent upon God for the very capacity to embrace the gospel, then clearly faith can contribute nothing to our salvation.

[49]

There are sound arguments for this interpretation, which completely rules out 'the most refined doctrine of conditional merit' (G. C. Berkouwer, *Faith and Justification*. p. 490). To insist that 'that' is neuter and 'faith' is feminine is not decisive against this view, which recognizes an advance in Paul's reasoning; whereas he merely repeats himself if 'that' is referred to 'salvation' rather than 'faith'. To say: 'You are saved by faith; not of yourselves; your salvation is the gift of God; it is not of works,' is simply to say the same thing without making any progress. But to say: 'You are saved through faith (and that not of yourselves it is the gift of God), not of works,' greatly increases the force of the passage (Charles Hodge).

*V*9: **not of works, that no man should glory.**

This is a familiar Pauline antithesis. It is an axiom of his gospel that God's grace leaves no room for man's merit, so that all boasting is absolutely excluded. That the glory of this salvation 'belongs wholly to God and in no degree to man, and that it has been so planned and so effected as to take from us all ground for boasting, is enforced on Paul's hearers again and again, in different connections, with anxious concern and utmost plainness of expression [cf *Rom* 3.27; 1 *Cor* 1.29, 4.7; *Gal* 6.14; *Phil* 3.3, etc.]' (Salmond).

*V*10: **For we are his workmanship, created in Christ Jesus for good works, which God afore prepared that we should walk in them.**

The proof that salvation is 'not of works' is given in the emphatic affirmation: '*his* workmanship (*poiēma*) are we.' The only other occurrence of this word in the New Testament is in *Rom* 1.20, where it refers to the natural creation ('the things that are made'); whereas here it is used of the new creation [cf *v* 15; 4.24]. As Christians owe their very existence to God's re-creative fiat, they can glory in nothing but the handiwork of grace. So Paul triumphantly exclaims, *He* has made us what we are!

But though salvation is not *of* works, yet we are created anew *for* good works, 'just as a tree may be said to be created for its fruit' (Alford). This ability to do those works which God adjudges to be good is not native to ourselves, for it is only 'in Christ Jesus' that this miraculous renewal has taken place [2 *Cor* 5.17]. And as such good works are the indispensable *evidence* of new life, this text must banish all slothfulness and stir us to earnest endeavour [*Rom* 12.1]. There is no excuse for indolence when God has previously prepared even the very works for our performance! God long before made ready our course of well-doing, so that we are in no position to boast of the good works that flow from our union with Christ. There is no need to prepare the works at this late date; all we need do is to walk in them. 'All the works are ready, they only await the living doers and their doing' (Lenski).

*V*11: **Wherefore remember, that once ye, the Gentiles in the flesh, who are called Uncircumcision by that which is called Circumcision, in the flesh, made by hands;**

In this section Paul reaches the very heart of his message, as he explains how Christ our peacemaker secured the unity of the church by that sacrifice which abolished the age-old enmity between Jews and Gentiles [*vv* 11-12].

Wherefore remember, As those who were once pagan Gentiles, the readers are here exhorted to remember with gratitude the great change that grace has wrought in their condition [*v* 12], and especially to reflect upon the marvellous difference their new standing before God has made in their relations with Jews who share their faith in Christ.

**that formerly ye Gentiles in the flesh called (in con-
tempt) Uncircumcision by the so-called Circumcision
in the flesh, a circumcision merely physical, made with
hands** (Abbott).

This puts Jews and Gentiles on exactly the same level of need
so that neither party can lord it over the other. The heathen
Gentiles were despised by the Jews for being outside the pale
of God's covenant; while the Jews, though in touch with the
means of grace, had not profited from their privileges because
they trusted in the outward sign of the covenant [*Rom* 2.28,
29], knowing nothing of that circumcision of the heart of
which the prophets spoke [*Deut* 10.16; *Jer* 4.4]. Yet in Christ
both Jews and Gentiles now know the blessed spiritual reality
of the 'circumcision made without hands' [*Col* 2.11], by which
they have become members of the same body [*vv* 14–18].
The fact is that in Christ Jesus 'neither circumcision availeth
anything, nor uncircumcision but a new creature' [*Gal* 6.15].

*V*12: **that ye were at that time separate from Christ,
alienated from the commonwealth of Israel, and strangers from the covenants of the promise, having no hope
and without God in the world.**

that ye were at that time separate from Christ, This is
what has well been called 'the first tragic predicate'. Paul calls
upon them to remember that in their former heathen state
they had no connection with Christ, for unlike the Jews they
did not look for the coming of the Messiah. Thus their complete separation from Christ, without whom there is no salvation, was the foundation of all the other miseries described
in the four following clauses.

alienated from the commonwealth of Israel, As alien Gentiles they were without the privileges of citizenship within the chosen community to whom God had made himself known 'in many and various ways' [*Heb* 1.1 RSV]. And this exclusion from Israel, the sole recipient of the light of God's special revelation [*Rom* 3.2], left them in the darkness of nature's night.

and strangers from the covenants of the promise, Consequently at that time they were ignorant of the *one* promise of salvation which God had confirmed to Abraham and his seed in several covenants. The one-sided character of these testaments of grace is shown by the fact that they are never called anything but *God's*, never Abraham's covenant or Israel's covenant!

having no hope This means that they were utterly without hope. They were engulfed by despair because they had no hope beyond the fragile tenure of their house of clay. It was this blank finality of death that robbed their present existence of any meaning. Hence they either squandered their days in cynical scepticism or 'squalid profligacy'.

and without God in the world. This was the 'deepest stage' of their misery, for though they believed in the gods of their own invention, they were destitute of the true knowledge of God [*John* 17.3]. For every man who is not taught by God's Word 'builds and forges absurd conceits of his own, and we know that man's mind is like a store of idolatry and superstition; so much so that if a man believes his own mind it is certain that he will forsake God and forge some idol in his own brain' (Calvin) [*Gal* 4.8].

*V*13: **But now in Christ Jesus ye that once were far off are made nigh in the blood of Christ.**

[53]

But now in Christ Jesus Another 'but' [cf *v* 4] marks the amazing contrast between their former lost condition and their present privileges in Christ *Jesus*, the personal name being added here to emphasize their personal interest in him as Saviour.

ye that once were far off are made nigh The words are taken from *Is* 57.19 [cf also *v* 17], and 'were frequently used by Rabbinic writers with reference to proselytes, who were said to be "brought near" ' (Abbott). Such converts merely came over from paganism to Judaism, but in Christ Jesus these Gentile believers had been brought into fellowship with God himself.

in the blood of Christ. By this one sacrifice for sin, Gentiles who were 'far off' and Jews who were 'nigh' [*v* 17], are both reconciled to God in that blood of the new covenant which has made them fellow-citizens in the same commonwealth of grace. Once again the word 'blood' bears eloquent testimony to the infinite cost of this reconciliation [1.7]. Indeed the whole gospel is centred upon it, for 'apart from shedding of blood there is no remission' [*Heb* 9.22]. Thus nothing less than the blood of the Surety shed in vicarious sacrifice was required to redeem his spiritual seed [*Is* 53.10–12; *Mark* 10.45; *Acts* 20.28].

*V*14: **For he is our peace, who made both one, and brake down the middle wall of partition,**
*V*15: **having abolished in his flesh the enmity, *even* the law of commandments *contained* in ordinances; that he might create in himself of the two one new man, *so* making peace;**

For he is our peace, who made both one, 'For' shows that the implications of the previous verse are about to be explained [*vv* 14–18]. Paul does not merely say that peace is the result of Christ's death, but confesses on behalf of all believing Jews and Gentiles that the risen Lord is in his own person '*our* peace'. 'Made both one' points to the definite act by which this peace was procured, though Christ's 'separated' members only enter into the experience of their unity through faith in the promise [cf *Gal* 3.26–29].

and has broken down the dividing wall of hostility, (RSV) Paul probably alludes to the wall in Herod's temple beyond which no Gentile might pass on pain of death, because the very fact that he was now a prisoner in Rome had arisen from the false charge of having taken Trophimus, an Ephesian, past this barrier [*Acts* 21.29]. It is no argument against this to say that the wall was still standing when this letter was written. For Paul could see in the union of Jews and Gentiles 'in one body' [*v* 16] that Christ's death had already broken down the hostility of which that barrier was the visible symbol. As the apostle to the Gentiles [3.1ff], he realized more clearly than anyone else that this mutual hatred was formed by the dividing wall of the law [*v* 15], which fenced off the Jews from the rest of mankind. To the Jews the law was the bastion of their privileges from which they looked down on the 'unclean' Gentiles with unmingled contempt; while to the Gentiles it was the outlandish rampart of an assumed superiority behind which 'the enemies of the human race' practised their abominable rites. Their reconciliation was therefore a miracle of grace, and that was objectively achieved when Christ broke down this wall of Jewish particularism [cf *Mark* 15.38]. For when he secured their peace with God he also united them in the bond of peace.

by abolishing in his flesh the law of commandments and ordinances, (RSV) Hodge's comment is very much to the point: 'The law was not abolished by Christ as a teacher; but by Christ as a sacrifice. It was not by his doctrine, but by his blood, his body, his death, his cross, that our deliverance from the law was effected. The doctrine of the passage, therefore, is that the middle wall of partition between Jews and Gentiles, consisting in their mutual enmity, has been removed by Christ's having, through his death, *abolished the law in all its forms, as a rule of justification*, and thus, opening one new way of access to God, common to Jews and Gentiles.' [cf *Rom* 10.3, 4: italics added].

that he might create in himself of the two one new man, *so* making peace; Christ's purpose in breaking down the hostility that divided Jew and Gentile was that he might create in himself 'one new man' [cf 4.13], a phrase which stands for the totality of the new creation as summed up in its Creator [2 *Cor* 5.17]. Thus it is by uniting Jew and Gentile in *one church* that Christ makes peace between them, having reconciled both to God [*v* 16].

*V*16: **and might reconcile them both in one body unto God through the cross, having slain the enmity thereby:**

From the consequences that Christ's death has for men Paul turns to the fundamental change it effected in their relation to God. It is only because God is reconciled to men through the propitiation of the cross that they can be at peace with one another, for it was there that Christ slew the divine enmity against sin which had resulted in their estrangement from God [cf 2.3; 5.5f]. 'His death satisfied justice, it propitiated God, i.e. removed his wrath, or his enmity to sinners; not hatred, for God is love, but the calm and holy purpose to punish them for their sins' (Charles Hodge).

The completeness of this reconciliation is indicated by the phrase 'in one body,' which does not refer to Christ's crucified body but to the church as his body [1.23]. This continued emphasis upon the corporate significance of Christ's objective achievement is important in showing that the church has an *ideal existence*, which is progressively realized as Jews and Gentiles are reconciled to God and to one another by the joyful discovery of their joint-membership within the one body of Christ [*vv* 17, 18].

*V*17: **and he came and preached peace to you that were far off, and peace to them that were nigh:**

After having explained the meaning of the cross, Paul does not leave us to imagine that the subjective application of the benefits Christ purchased by his death are then left to 'chance'! On the contrary, he expressly affirms that Christ himself is the preacher of this peace both to the 'far off' Gentiles and the Jews who were 'nigh'. And this he does, 'having come' as he promised in the Spirit [*John* 14.18], so that his voice continues to be heard through the authentic proclamation of the apostolic gospel [*Is* 57.19; *Rom* 10.15]. This divine initiative is indispensably necessary, for such is the inability of the natural man that ncithcr the pagan Gentiles nor the externally privileged Jews would ever have 'decided' to come to Christ – *he had to come to them*! ' "Go!" is still his command to us for our mission work. This going is his coming' (Lenski).

*V*18: **for through him we both have our access in one Spirit unto the Father:**

This teaches us that it is in communion with the Father that the great goal of reconciliation is reached. Although Paul previously spoke of the act which made of Jew and Gentile '*one new man*' [*v* 15], here he says 'we *both*' which acknowledges that the outward distinctions remain, though religiously they have ceased to matter [cf *Gal* 3.28]. For through the one Mediator [1 *Tim* 2.5] they both now enjoy the same access in one Spirit [1 *Cor* 12.13] to the one Father [4.6] – a statement which shows that the doctrine of the Trinity is not a dead dogma but a living development of the Christian experience of salvation. These privileges are vastly superior to those possessed by the Jews under the law, for then they had no right of immediate access to God and their worship lacked the filial confidence by which the gospel economy is characterized. 'As that right is ours only *through* Christ, so it is made ours in actual experience only *in* the Spirit, and Jew and Gentile have it alike because it is one and the same Spirit that works in both. So both have continuous access to God from whom once they were far removed, and to him, too, in the benign character of the *Father* whom they can approach without fear' (Salmond).

*V*19: **So then ye are no more strangers and sojourners, but ye are fellow-citizens with the saints, and of the household of God:**

'So then' introduces the conclusion that Paul would have his Gentile readers draw from the facts just adduced [*vv* 19–22]. For though they were once excluded from 'the commonwealth of Israel' [*v* 12], they are no longer 'strangers' – aliens without the rights of residence – or even 'sojourners' – tolerated outsiders living in a community to which they did not properly belong. Now that they are the free-born citizens of 'the Israel of God' [*Gal* 6.16] they have been placed on a level of perfect equality with 'the saints,' i.e. with all other believers, whatever their natural descent [*Gal* 3.9]. As Abbott says, 'The word does not refer to personal holiness, but to membership of the spiritual commonwealth to which Jewish and Gentile Christians alike belong'. And what is even more amazing, they have been brought into 'the household of faith' [*Gal* 6.10], not as servants or slaves, but as full members of the Father's family, his children by the adoption of grace!

'In any part of the Christian church all national distinctions are swept away, and we are no more foreigners and strangers, but fellow citizens of the saints and of the household of God ... God has levelled down the Jews and made them stand in the same class as the Gentiles ... He has levelled up the outcast and despised Gentiles and has admitted us to all the privileges of his ancient covenant, making us to be heirs of Abraham ... He has given us all the blessings which belong to Abraham's seed, because we, too, possess like precious faith as the father of the faithful himself had ... Oh, what a blessing it is that all racial, national, and ceremonial distinctions have gone forever, and that Christ is all in all to all who believe in him' (C. H. Spurgeon).

*V*20: **being built upon the foundation of the apostles and prophets, Christ Jesus himself being the chief corner stone;**

You are built upon the foundation laid by the apostles and prophets, (NEB). Paul here takes an important step forward in his development of the 'house' image. Advancing from the thought of family-members dwelling within God's household [*v* 19], he now sees the believing Gentiles as built into the very fabric of that house which is indwelt by God himself [*v* 22]. Thus in contrast to the provisional nature of temples made with hands [*Acts* 7.48], the New Temple (i.e. the church) is the permanent edifice because it is a living organism [1 *Pet* 2.5]. Although the Greek is ambiguous, it is preferable to understand the apostolic proclamation *of CHRIST* as the foundation upon which the church is built (the verb is a passive which points to God as the true author of this work). The unique task assigned to the apostles and prophets proves that they can have no successors today, for clearly this foundation could only be laid once [cf 1 *Cor* 3.10, 11]. Like the apostles with whom they are classed, the New Testament prophets [3.5; 4.11; *Acts* 13.1] also exercised an un-

[59]

repeatable function in that they spoke under the direct inspiration of the Spirit, 'and prior to the completion of the
canon they stood to those early churches in such a relation
as the written oracles stand to us' (Eadie).

and Christ Jesus himself is the foundation-stone. (NEB).
Many scholars explain this in terms of the key-stone which
holds the final arch of the building in place, but it seems more
appropriate to adhere to the traditional view of the foundation
stone. However, this is no ordinary foundation-stone because
the whole building *grows* out from it [*v* 21]. Paul may well
have had in mind the rabbinic tradition which regarded the
foundation-stone of Zion [*Is* 28.16] as the embryonic centre
from which God created the world. The physiological features falsely attributed to that stone can be truly predicated of
Christ as the foundation-stone of the church which is his new
creation. 'He creates it, sustains it, imparts harmony and unity
to it, just as he determines its "shape" and growth' (R. J.
McKelvey, *The New Temple*, p. 204).

*V*21: **in whom each several building, fitly framed together, groweth into a holy temple in the Lord;**

in whom all the building (AV), 'In whom each several
building' must be rejected because a multiplicity of buildings
is completely at odds with the thought of the passage, which
speaks only of two parts (Jew and Gentile) which are made
one. Hence Paul says that it is in Christ that the whole building, into which his Gentile readers have been incorporated, is
'being fitly joined together.' The only other occurrence of
this compound verb in the New Testament is found in 4.16,
where it more naturally refers to the harmonious growth of
the members of the body. But as the word was used of the
mason's art in preparing stones for the building this technical
meaning may be in view here.

In stating that the *building* is growing into a *temple*, Paul does not mean that the church will not become a temple until its growth is complete. For, as McKelvey suggests, we have here two distinct images which convey two different ideas. 'Viewed as the building the church is still under construction; viewed as the temple, however, it is an inhabited dwelling' (*The New Temple*, p. 117). In the church there is the *spiritual* fulfilment of what was signified by the inner sanctuary of the temple in Jerusalem, for the glory of God is manifested among the redeemed who are a *holy* community in virtue of their vital union with the Lord.

*V*22: **in whom ye also are builded together for a habitation of God in the Spirit.**

And it is in Christ that 'ye also' – you Gentiles as well as believing Jews – 'are being built together' (compound verb found only here in the New Testament) into a habitation of God which is realized *in* the Spirit. Paul is not enforcing a duty; he is describing the greatness of their privilege as constituent members of God's habitation. No higher view of the church is possible, but we are intended to reach this height and not fall sadly short of it! 'The Father makes choice of this house, the Son purchaseth it, the Holy Ghost taketh possession of it. This happiness he best understandeth that most feeleth. The cock on the dunghill knows it not' (Trapp).

CHAPTER THREE

This truth that the Gentiles are equal heirs with Jews of the same inheritance was hidden from former generations, but now has been revealed to the apostles and prophets; and Paul, despite his own unworthiness, has been entrusted with the key rôle of preaching Christ to the Gentiles, and of making known this mystery to all men [vv 1–9]. It was God's eternal purpose that even the angelic powers should come to know his many-splendoured wisdom through the church in which all the redeemed are united in their Redeemer [vv 10–12]. Paul's prayer for his readers is that they might be given the inner spiritual strength and steadfast love which would lead to a greater knowledge of the love of Christ, even though this can never be fully comprehended. He concludes with another doxology to God for the manifestation of his power in the church [vv 13–21].

V1: For this cause I Paul, the prisoner of Christ Jesus in behalf of you Gentiles,—

So far the Epistle has been strangely impersonal, for Paul has been wholly taken up with God's great salvation and the Gentiles' part in it. 'It is only as he reaches a resting-place in his thought, that he hears as it were the clink of his chain, and remembers where he is and why he is there: *I Paul, the prisoner of Christ Jesus for you, the Gentiles*' (J. Armitage Robinson). At this point the construction is broken as the apostle pauses to explain the significance of his ministry [*vv*

2–13], before resuming the thread with a repeated 'for this cause' in verse 14.

Paul wishes his imprisonment to be understood in terms of persons: he serves *Christ* by ministering to the *Gentiles*. He is not ashamed to confess that he is a 'prisoner' in such an honourable cause, but he does not regard himself as Caesar's captive. He is *Christ's* prisoner: 1. Because he knows that he is not detained at Caesar's pleasure, 2. Because he belongs to Christ no less in captivity than when he is at liberty [*Rom* 8.35f]. The Ephesians ought to be among the first to acknowledge that Paul is a prisoner for the sake of Gentile freedom, for his arrest in Jerusalem followed the uproar caused by the false charge that he had taken with him into the temple an Ephesian believer named Trophimus [*Acts* 21.29].

V2: **if so be that ye have heard of the dispensation of that grace of God which was given me to you-ward;**

for surely you have heard ... (NEB) The expression Paul uses assumes that his readers *have* heard, though it is vague enough to cover those who have *only* heard (e.g. converts who joined the church after he left Ephesus, and believers in other churches). As in *Col* 1.25 'the dispensation' was the stewardship that God gave to Paul along with the requisite grace to fulfil it. He neither received the office from man, nor did he preach according to his own wisdom. For though men may take to themselves the name of 'apostle', the fact that they so conspicuously lack 'the signs of an apostle' shows that this is a mere sham without substance. Moreover, this grace was not a private gift for Paul to keep to himself [cf 4.12]; it was bestowed upon him for the benefit of the Gentiles. After surveying Paul's use of the word 'grace' in connection with his ministry to the Gentiles, J. Armitage Robinson concludes that it is impossible to doubt that it is 'dominated by the thought of the admission of the Gentiles to the privileges which had been peculiar to Israel. Grace was given to the Gentiles through his ministry: grace was given to him for his ministry to them'.

V3: **how that by revelation was made known unto me the mystery, as I wrote before in few words,**

Paul is about to explain the mystery to which he referred at the beginning of the Epistle (see note on 1.9), but even now he holds back the disclosure of what this mystery is until its dramatic announcement in verse 6. The apostle's reticence is no mere literary device; his purpose is to draw forth the adoring wonder of the Gentiles for the surpassing riches of God's grace towards them. Saul the Pharisee was such an extraordinary choice for *the* apostle to the heathen that nothing could have fitted him for this office but that overwhelming revelation on the Damascus road which secured his unconditional surrender to the divine will [*Gal* 1.16]. It was therefore 'by special instruction that he comprehended the worldwide adaptations of the gospel, and gave himself to the work of evangelizing the heathen' (Eadie) [*Acts* 22.21].

as I have written above in brief, (Moule). The reference is not to some previous letter, but to the immediately preceding paragraphs in which he urged his Gentile readers to remember what they were and what they have now become, equal members with Jewish Christians of the one church of God [2.11–22].

V4: **whereby, when ye read, ye can perceive my understanding in the mystery of Christ;**

Paul is therefore confident that as they read what he has written above they will perceive his insight into 'the mystery of Christ', i.e. his inspired interpretation of the gospel through which the meaning of this mystery is revealed. Verse 8 confirms that there is nothing boastful in this statement; Paul is simply drawing attention to the significance of what has been committed to him. For it is incredible that the recipient of such a revelation would be unaware of its supreme value, and would take no pains to impress its importance upon those to whom he was authorized to communicate it. In writing to the Colossians who were confronted by the perils of a false 'gnosis' Paul was concerned to stress that aspect of the mystery which would counteract these claims, *viz.* the personal in-dwelling of Christ in every believer [*Col* 1.27]; whereas in this letter he brings out the corporate dimensions of the mystery, *viz.* that Christ is the Head of the church in which Jews and Gentiles are united as fellow-members of the same body.

V5: **which in other generations was not made known unto the sons of men, as it hath now been revealed unto his holy apostles and prophets in the Spirit;**

The privileges of living in the age of gospel grace are great indeed, for this mystery was not made known to men of former generations as clearly as it has now been revealed by the Spirit to his apostles and prophets (see note on 2.20). There is beautiful parallelism in this statement – temporal, reve-lational, and personal –

which in other generations	**as it hath now**
was not made known	**been revealed**
unto the sons of men,	**unto his holy apostles**
	and prophets.

Critics have seized upon the word 'holy' as un-Pauline, but a glance at the above arrangement will suffice to show that there is no incongruity in describing the apostles and prophets as 'holy' when they are contrasted with the rest of mankind ('the sons of men'). That the Gentiles were to be included within the scope of divine blessing was the promise first given to Abraham and repeatedly confirmed throughout the Old Testament, but that its fulfilment would make of Jews and Gentiles 'one new man' was a truth so astonishing that it could not be disclosed until their reconciliation had been objectively secured (2.16, 17: cf Denney's remark: Reconciliation 'is a work which is *finished*, and which we must conceive to be finished, *before the gospel is preached*'). And not even these apostles and prophets of the new covenant would have received the Gentiles into the church on equal terms with the Jews without the evident persuasion of the promised Spirit [*Acts* 10.44, 45; 11.15–17; 15. 8–12].

*V*6: *to wit*, **that the Gentiles are fellow-heirs, and fellow-members of the body, and fellow-partakers of the promise in Christ Jesus through the gospel,**

Here Paul at last makes an explicit declaration of the content of this long-hidden mystery. It is that the Gentiles are *fellow*-heirs with the Jews, being *fellow*-members with them of the body, and *fellow*-partakers with them of the promised salvation [another triad of compounds beginning with *syn*: cf. 2.5, 6]. 1. 'Fellow-heirs' means that though their interest in the inheritance was only recently revealed, yet theirs was no second-rate blessing for they inherited equally with the earlier sons. 2. 'Fellow-members' was coined by Paul and it means 'concorporate'. 'In relation to the Body, the members are "incorporate": in relation to one another they are "concorporate", that is, sharers in the one Body' (J. Armitage Robinson). 3. 'Fellow-partakers shows that they are now 'joint-sharers' in 'those covenant-promises from which they had once been excluded [2.12]' (Bruce).

in Christ Jesus through the gospel, All these privileges are now enjoyed by the Gentiles '*in* Christ Jesus', for the sole de-

positary of salvation is the One in whom it was objectively
accomplished; but it was '*through* the gospel', the preaching
of the good news, that they actually entered into the possession of this salvation – a fact which highlights the importance
of preaching [*v* 7].

*V*7: **whereof I was made a minister, according to the
gift of that grace of God which was given me according
to the working of his power.**

Unworthy and unfitted as he was for the work, Paul nevertheless became a minister of his gospel by the gift of that grace
which so powerfully equipped him for God's service. His
commission to preach the gospel to the Gentiles was the gift
of God's grace, even as the ability to fulfil that ministry
called for the mighty energizing of God's power. For to trans-
form 'a Jew into a Christian, a blasphemer into a saint, a
Pharisee into an apostle, and a persecutor into a missionary'
was such a change as could only be wrought by the omnipotence of grace [1.19] (Eadie). We must learn from this that
the true and able ministers of the new covenant are not self-
appointed, for it is by God's grace that they are called and
empowered to preach the gospel. So, 'let us at this day understand that whenever it pleases God to raise up men of skill
who have the gift of teaching us, it is a sure indication that he
has pitied us already, and intends to call us to the inheritance
of salvation' (Calvin).

*V*8: **Unto me, who am less than the least of all saints,
was this grace given, to preach unto the Gentiles the
unsearchable riches of Christ;**

Some scholars see the hand of an imitator in this profound
expression of self-abasement, but those with saner judgment
insist that the utterance is entirely characteristic of the apostle.

The shameful remembrance of his career as a persecutor is quite sufficient to account for it [cf 1 *Tim* 1.12–16]. It does not really go beyond 1 *Cor* 15.9; 'for there he declares himself not only the least of the apostles, but not meet to be called an apostle; here he does not say that he is not meet to be reckoned amongst the saints' (Abbott). So though he accounts himself as 'less than the least', he still claims to be a saint!

Paul thus regards it as the greatest mark of grace that he was given the task of preaching to the Gentiles, whose complete bankruptcy presented no problem to the One whose resources are illimitable [cf *Rom* 11.33]. These 'unfathomable' riches of Christ 'are the fulness of the Godhead, the plenitude of all divine glories and perfections which dwell in him; the fulness of grace to pardon, to sanctify and save; every thing in short, which renders him the satisfying portion of the soul' (Charles Hodge).

*V*9: **and to make all men see what is the dispensation of the mystery which for ages hath been hid in God who created all things;**

and to make all men see what is the plan of the mystery hidden for ages in God who created all things; (RSV) Another purpose of Paul's preaching is to enlighten all men (Jews as well as Gentiles) through the setting forth of God's eternal plan of redemption. This is the mystery which for ages has been hidden in God, that is to say, from the moment that there were any created intelligences from whom it could be concealed. It is this age-long concealment which makes the present revelation of the mystery of such momentous importance for all mankind [*Heb* 2.3]. It is vital to grasp the fact that there is nothing provisional or temporary about the gospel. It is God's last word to men. Hence its publication is *the* eschatological event which ushers in the period of the end-time [*Rom* 16.25, 26]. Paul was so acutely conscious of the absolute *finality* of the gospel that he addresses those who are privileged to live in the days of its disclosure as the ones 'upon whom the ends of the ages are come' [1 *Cor* 10.11]. And in case any are inclined to find fault with the timing of this revelation, Paul here adds that it is God 'who created *all things*', since this is 'a fact which involves his perfect right to adjust all things as he will' (Alford).

*V*10: **to the intent that now unto the principalities and the powers in the heavenly *places* might be made known through the church the manifold wisdom of God,**

In verse 8 Paul contrasted the greatness of his calling with his own unworthiness, and then showed that the design of his mission was to preach to the Gentiles and to enlighten all men concerning the long-hidden mystery of redemption. And now he states that this takes place in order that the church thus formed might now furnish the heavenly world with a dazzling display of the 'many-splendoured wisdom of God' (Bruce). That good angels are meant is suggested by the exalted nature of the passage, and confirmed by the thought that 'evil angels more naturally recognize the *power*, good angels the *wisdom* of God' (Ellicott). The amazing announcement that even the angels obtain the knowledge of God's wisdom 'through the church' should surely give us pause for thought. For it is in the New Testament *ecclesia* – chosen by God, redeemed by Christ, and sanctified by the Spirit – that there is at last revealed to the angels' wondering gaze the consummation of God's eternal purpose [cf 1 *Pet* 1.12]. 'In different ways had God dealt with men, with the Jew in one way and with the Gentile in another, in the long course of the ages. But in all these he had had one great end in view. Now in the *church* the realization of that end is seen, and in that great spiritual harmony angels can perceive the manifoldness and majesty of that divine wisdom which by ways so diverse had been working to this great result' (Salmond).

*V*11: **according to the eternal purpose which he purposed in Christ Jesus our Lord:**

When Paul sees in the establishment of the church nothing less than the fulfilment of God's eternal purpose, then it is clearly something more than a mere 'parenthesis' in the plan of God! In contrast to the theories of men, Scripture teaches that nothing can succeed that which stands at the climax of redemptive history [cf *Heb* 12.22–24]. 'The past *ages*, angelic, paradisaic, patriarchal, Mosaic, prophetic, have led up to the Universal Church, in its spiritual reality, as their goal' (Moule). **which he purposed in Christ Jesus our Lord:** Although some recent versions give the verb 'made' the historical sense of 'wrought out' (e.g. RSV: 'realized'), it is preferable to take it as meaning that God 'formed' this eternal purpose in him whom we know as 'Christ Jesus our Lord', since the tense would appear to point back to the origination of that grand design.

*V*12: **in whom we have boldness and access in confidence through our faith in him.**

The experimental character of Paul's concluding affirmation shows why he chose to use the full title, 'Christ Jesus our Lord', in the previous verse. For he would not have us forget that it is only 'in him' that we can approach God in the confidence that we have 'boldness and access'. This is the openness of children before their Father [2.18], and it is realized through our faith in Christ, who is himself the objective ground of that privilege. Thus, 'we may always come boldly to God's throne, assuring ourselves that his majesty will no more be terrifying to us, seeing he shows himself a Father towards us in the person of his only Son. We see then that St. Paul's intention is to keep us close to Jesus Christ' (Calvin).

Paul's masterly survey of the significance of his work

among the Gentiles within the plan of God is helpfully summarized by Lenski as follows:

1. The divine purpose going back to eternity.
2. Formed in Christ Jesus, our Lord.
3. Standing veiled in all past ages yet standing nonetheless.
4. Revealed in gospel preaching to all men including the Gentiles.
5. Establishing the church of the New Testament with its wonderful universality.
6. Unveiling even to the angels in heaven the wonderful wisdom of God contained in the divine purpose from its inception onward.
7. Putting us believers into possession of the enjoyment of the highest earthly communion with our heavenly Father.

V13: **Wherefore I ask that ye may not faint at my tribulations for you, which are your glory.**

The greatness of Paul's heart is shown by the measure of his concern for his readers. As Christ's prisoner for the Gentiles he can glory in tribulations [3.1], so he gives no thought to himself. Instead he asks that they may not lose heart at what he endures on their behalf! In fact if they share his perspective they will see that these tribulations are their glory, for it was in the worthwhile cause of securing their freedom that his liberty had been sacrificed. So they must not become discouraged as though the Gentile mission were disgraced rather than advanced by his sufferings. Indeed this Epistle was the proof that their apostle could minister a special blessing to them, and the whole church of God, even from a Roman prison.

V14: **For this cause I bow my knees unto the Father,**

*V*15: **from whom every family in heaven and on earth is named,**

'For this cause' harks back to verse 1, where the phrase refers to the preceding exposition of the unity of Jews and Gentiles in one body through the cross [2.11–22]. And now, after having explained his part in this great work [*vv* 2–13], Paul again follows teaching by prayer [*vv* 14–21; cf 1.15–23]. 'He mentions his prayers for them, not only to testify his love for them, but also that they themselves may pray. For the Word is sown in vain, unless the Lord fertilizes it by his blessing. Therefore let pastors learn from Paul's example, not only to admonish and exhort people, but also to seek from the Lord success for their labours, that they may not be unfruitful' (Calvin, *Commentary*). Although standing was the usual posture for prayer among the Jews [*Matt* 6.5; *Luke* 18.11, 13], the urgent intensity of Paul's supplication is indicated by the words 'I bow my knees unto the Father' [cf *Luke* 22.41; *Acts* 20.36, 21.5].

of whom the whole family in heaven and earth is named

(AV). Many scholars claim that the absence of the article demands the translation 'every family', but C. F. D. Moule rightly hesitates to accept this ruling and claims that 2 *Tim* 3.16 'is most unlikely to mean *every inspired scripture*, and much more probably means *the whole scripture (is) inspired*'. In this case 'the whole family' is required by the context, which has the unity of the church as its dominant concept [cf 2.14, 16, 18, 19, 21; 3.6]. In view of the apostle's unwearied insistence upon this fact, it would be very strange if he now began to speak of a multiplicity of families, thus raising but not resolving interesting speculations about the 'angelic' families in heaven! What Paul has in mind is the entire company of the redeemed which makes up 'the Father's family' (Hendriksen). 'The name this great family bears always indicates its Father.

This family is the *Una Sancta*. A part of it is already in heaven, the other part is still on earth' (Lenski).

*V*16: **that he would grant you, according to the riches of his glory, that ye may be strengthened with power through his Spirit in the inward man;**
*V*17a: **that Christ may dwell in your hearts through faith;**

Here we have the content of what many consider to be the most sublime of all Paul's prayers. 'The riches of his glory, are the sum of God's manifested perfections, not merely his grace or his power, but all his attributes as these are harmoniously exercised in the salvation of his people. Thus the 'measure of the gift for which Paul prays on behalf of the Ephesians is nothing short of those perfections of God which are revealed now in their glorious fulness and inexhaustible wealth [cf 1.7, 18; 2.4, 7]' (Salmond).

It is evident from this prayer that conversion is but the beginning of the work of grace in the believer. The apostle did not regard the seal of the Spirit as an end in itself, but as the guarantee of continued spiritual progress [1.13, 14]. He therefore prays that those who have received this initial bestowment of grace may be further strengthened 'with power through his Spirit' [see also comment on 5.18]. The Christian 'has not yet begun to conceive of the rich heritage unto which God has begotten him unless he perceives that it is his privilege, his duty, his rightful portion, to be strong with the strength of the divine Spirit. The devil seeks to persuade us that God would have his children remain frail and feeble in this life, but that is one of his many lies. God's revealed will for us is the very reverse, namely, "Be strong in the Lord, and in the power of his might" [6.10]' (Pink).

'The inward man' is neither the soul as opposed to the body, nor the rational as distinguished from the sensual principle of life; it is the essential man who delights in the law of God [Rom 7.22], the hidden self whose daily renewal is contrasted with the declining powers of the outward man [2 Cor 4.16]. But as Paul nowhere represents the renewing as an automatic process, he prays that the indwelling presence of Christ may be realized 'through faith', for even the subjective side of salvation depends upon this further gift of grace [2.8; Phil 1.29].

Calvin has some searching words on the importance of a real heart knowledge of Christ: 'For many men have him in their mouth, and even also in their brain, as they hear him, and they think they acquit themselves well when they can prattle about him, but in the meanwhile there is no living root in them. It is not enough then to have some vague knowledge of Christ, or to engage in airy speculations, as they say, and to be able to talk a lot about him, but he must have his seat in our hearts within, so that we are unfeignedly joined to him, and with true affection. That is the way for us to be partakers of God's Spirit'.

V17b: **to the end that ye, being rooted and grounded in love,**
V18: **may be strong to apprehend with all the saints what is the breadth and length and height and depth,**
V19a: **and to know the love of Christ which passeth knowledge,**

Paul mixes his metaphors but his meaning is plain. So basic is the grace of love to the Christian that it may be compared with the roots of a tree or the foundation of a building [cf Col 2.7 and NEB: 'deep roots and firm foundations']. This doubling of participles emphasizes the primacy of love, just as the perfect tense points to the establishment and continuance in love as the essential condition for an increase in our knowledge of Christ's love. Between our spiritual strengthening and the enlargement of our spiritual understanding there is an intermediate link of love. 'The Spirit does not immediately work this enlargement of mind in us; he immediately works love, and only through working this love, enlarges our apprehension. The Holy Ghost "sheds love abroad in our hearts." Love is the great enlarger. It is love which stretches the intellect. He who is not filled with love is necessarily small, withered, shrivelled in his outlook on life and things. And conversely he who is filled with love is large and copious in his apprehensions. Only he can apprehend with all saints what is the breadth and length and height and depth of things' (B. B. Warfield, *Faith and Life*, pp. 275–6).

may be strong to apprehend with all the saints what is the breadth and length and height and depth, and to know the love of Christ which passeth knowledge, It is Paul's desire that the Ephesians, not as an isolated community but in company with all believers, may be fully able to comprehend the immensity of that love which is far beyond their knowledge! The solution to this paradox lies in taking note of the difference between what is possible and impossible. Paul prays for an increasing *experimental* knowledge of Christ's love because it is not unknowable; but he also recognizes that finite souls can never possess an *exhaustive* knowledge of an infinite love. Despite the misdirected ingenuity of some patristic interpreters, no mystical meaning may be imposed upon the four different dimensions, which 'are introduced with no other purpose than the simple and consistent one of setting forth the surpassing magnitude of Christ's love for us' (Salmond).

*V*19b: **that ye may be filled unto all the fulness of God.**

The words which form this astonishing climax are easy to read, but who can fathom their meaning? Yet at least we should not allow our familiarity with the words to blunt our appreciation of the boundless nature of Paul's concluding request. It is that they may be filled 'unto' all the fulness of God, a preposition which 'suggests the idea of a continuous process, a progressive and enlarging experience' (Pink). This is no unattainable ideal, but the great goal which is to be realized in union with Christ, through whom alone the divine fulness can be communicated to the sons of men [*Col* 2.9]. 'Absolute perfection is the standard to which the believer is to attain. He is predestinated to be conformed to the image of the Son of God, *Rom* 8.29. He is to be perfect as man, as God is perfect as God; and the perfection of man consists in his being full of God; God dwelling in him so as absolutely to control all his cognitions, feelings, and outward actions' (Charles Hodge) [cf 4.13]. This therefore means that even when he is eventually filled with all the fulness of God, man does not himself become divine but remains a creature whose glory consists in eternally reflecting the glory of his Creator.

*V*20: **Now unto him that is able to do exceeding abundantly above all that we ask or think, according to the power that worketh in us,**
*V*21: **unto him** *be* **the glory in the church and in Christ Jesus unto all generations for ever and ever. Amen.**

Now to him who is able to do infinitely more than all we ask or imagine, (Hendriksen). In the final petition the limits of human thought and language were reached, but no such limitation can be placed upon God's infinite resources. In this magnificent doxology Paul therefore gives sublime expression to the truth that God not only has absolute ability, but that he exercises that ability towards believers in a manner which far transcends their highest aspirations and utmost imaginings. Paul uses the compound 'infinitely more' (*huperek-perissou*) because nothing less than this intensified superlative is adequate to describe the fulness of God [*v* 19] which is now freely poured out, on the ground of Christ's finished work [4.8], in the gift of the Spirit ('according to the power that worketh in us').

according to the power that worketh in us, 'Those who have been raised from the dead, who have been transformed by the renewing of their minds, translated from the kingdom of darkness into the kingdom of God's dear Son, and in whom God himself dwells by his Spirit, having already experienced a change which nothing but omnipotence could effect, may well join in the doxology to him who is able to do exceeding abundantly above all we can ask or think' (Hodge).

unto him *be* the glory in the church and in Christ Jesus, God is the one to whom all glory belongs, but it is only because he was pleased to manifest that glory to the praise of his *grace* that we can glorify him as we ought. Thus Paul says, Let God be glorified 'in the church', for the community of the redeemed is the body of Christ; 'and in Christ Jesus', the divine Head of the church who alone makes its praise acceptable to God.

unto all generations for ever and ever. Amen. The meaning of this remarkable expression appears to be that the church's praise shall endure throughout the present age 'unto all generations' of believers, and then throughout the ages to come (i.e. to all eternity). 'Amen' in Scripture indicates far more than intellectual assent. 'It always involves an energetic

[77]

demand for faith since it seals something that pertains to Christ and salvation' (Lenski). Therefore if we would truly endorse the promise of God in Christ our 'Amens' must register the ardent conviction of our hearts.

CHAPTER FOUR

This begins the practical section of the Epistle in which the apostle exhorts believers to live as befits their high calling in Christ (ch. 4–6). They must be careful to cherish the graces of lowliness, patience, and love, which make it possible to maintain the unity of the Spirit. For the church is one body, having one hope, inspired by one Spirit, acknowledging one Lord, one faith, one baptism, and one Father of all [vv 1–6]. This unity is not achieved by a drab uniformity, but through the ascended Christ's bestowal of a rich diversity of gifts, all of which are designed to edify the church [vv 7–13]. Instead of being unsettled by the shifting stratagems of error, believers are to attain spiritual maturity by speaking the truth in love, so that they will receive through the appropriate contribution of each member such nourishment from Christ their Head that the whole body will be built up in love [vv 14–16]. With this great end in view, they are to abandon the patterns of thought and conduct which characterized the old life, and remembering that they have put on the new man, they must now live by new standards [vv 17–24]. This means discarding the things which grieve the Holy Spirit, especially lying, anger, stealing, and harmful speech; and replacing them with kindness and gentleness as found in God's treatment of them in Christ [vv 25–32].

V1: **I therefore, the prisoner of the Lord, beseech you to walk worthily of the calling wherewith ye were called,**

The second part of the Epistle begins with this chapter. And as usual in Paul, 'therefore' marks the logical transition from doctrine to its practical application in the lives of believers [cf *Rom* 12.1; *Col* 3.1; 1 *Thess* 4.1]. It should be noted that Paul neither dragoons his readers into submission, nor cajoles them by flattery, but always *appeals* for the obedience their gospel-allegiance demands, for such is the mode of address that befits those who are the children of the King.

In 3.1 Paul refers to Christ as the author and originator of his captivity, but here he regards it as the consequence of his union with Christ and of his devotion in his service. Hence it is as the Lord's *faithful* prisoner that he exhorts them to walk 'worthily' of their high calling [*Col* 1.10]. This comprehensive principle offers us sure guidance in all doubtful situations which are not covered by specific precepts: 'which course of action will be most worthy of the calling with which God has called us?' (Bruce).

'The calling which is wholly of God comes first, and a corresponding life is looked for as the fitting and appropriate fruit of that calling. Their walking can never render them worthy of the calling of God which is theirs of free grace; but having been enlightened and strengthened, as Paul had prayed that they might be, they are to bring forth fruits in the life, which will give evidence of the presence of the Holy Spirit and the indwelling of Christ in their hearts' (Macpherson).

*V*2: **with all lowliness and meekness, with longsuffering, forbearing one another in love;**
*V*3: **giving diligence to keep the unity of the Spirit in the bond of peace.**

In verse 2 Paul states four graces which should attend this walk, and in verse 3 specifies the particular direction in which they are to be exercised. Believers are to walk 'with *all* lowliness and meekness', for without humility of mind [*Phil* 2.3] and the forbearance that is inspired by love, they will not be able to bear 'with longsuffering' the faults and failings of others, and so 'keep the unity of the Spirit in the bond of peace' [cf *Phil* 4.2].

Lowliness found no place in heathen ethics since it was thought of as a form of abject grovelling. That it became a primary Christian virtue is entirely due to the example and teaching of Christ [*John* 13.4ff.], whose sinless humility consisted in taking the form of a servant and rendering a perfect obedience to God [*Phil* 2.5–8]. With us lowliness also consists in taking our proper place before God, but because we are sinners as he was not, in our case this means 'the esteeming of ourselves small, inasmuch as we are so; the thinking truly, and because truly, therefore lowlily, of ourselves' (Trench).

Meekness is again primarily meekness towards God; it is not weakness but the grace which is the opposite of all self-assertiveness. For it is in submitting ourselves to God that we are given the strength to serve others. Longsuffering and forbearance are both divine perfections which are to find their finite reflection in us. As God is slow to anger, so we are to be longsuffering by enduring provocations without quickly giving way to passion. And this is made possible by a loving forbearance that is the fruit of God's gracious dealings with us.

It is in this way that believers are to make every effort to preserve that unity already established by the Spirit in the bond of peace. As 'the unity of the Spirit' is the gift which enables men to recognize one another as members of the same body, so 'the bond of peace' inevitably recalls the objective achievement by which their reconciliation was secured. 'That "peace" with God, and in him with one another, which is in fact Christ himself [2.14], in his sacrifice and his presence, is to form the "bond" which shall maintain you in a holy union of spiritual hope and aim' (Moule).

*V*4: *There is* one body, and one Spirit, even as also ye were called in one hope of your calling;
*V*5: one Lord, one faith, one baptism;
*V*6: one God and Father of all, who is over all, and through all, and in all.

Having urged his readers to preserve their God-given unity, Paul immediately adds a sevenfold description of its unique basis, which may well echo an early confession of faith. He insists that *all* believers:

    (i) belong to *one body*, because they are indwelt by *one Spirit*, and are joined in *one hope;*
    (ii) are united with *one Lord* through *one faith* confessed in *one baptism*;
    (iii) have *one God and Father* who had made them the children of his grace.

1. **one body** The one body is the one church of Christ. It remains an invisible body to the extent that it includes all Christ's members and excludes all false professors, but this does not mean that it is without any visible manifestation in the world. For the Lord adds to the church those whom he calls out from the world [*Acts* 2.47]. Thus when the elect in Corinth were converted they formed the church in that city [*Acts* 18.10, 11; 1 *Cor* 1.2]. And it was because Paul recognized the grace which had given them this corporate identity that he laboured to preserve its peace, purity, and unity. Yet it is *believers* who make up this body, and not the sum total of local visible churches. Thus because each member of the body is directly related to the Head, the church must never be regarded as a 'mediating institution' which comes between the soul and the Saviour (Edmund Clowney) [1 *Tim* 2.5].

2. one Spirit Just as the human body has many members which are joined together in virtue of its common life, so the unity of Christ's members in one body is realized through the one Spirit who indwells them all [2.18; *Rom* 8.9; 1 *Cor* 3.16]. 'This fact prevents any view of the church as a mere organization; for the presence of the Spirit constitutes the church, and is the basis of its unity' (Foulkes).

3. one hope Although they were once strangers without hope [2.12], the call of God's grace gave them the assured hope of an heavenly inheritance [1.18], a foretaste of which they had already received in the gift of the Spirit [1.14]. 'The fact that, when they were called out of heathenism, one and the same *hope* was born in them, is a fact in perfect keeping with the unity of the Christian body and the unity of the divine Spirit operating in it, and the one confirms and illumines the other' (Salmond).

4. one Lord In gladly confessing 'Jesus is Lord', the early Christians gave voice to the uniqueness of the Person in whom they had found their salvation [1 *Cor* 12.3; *Phil* 2.11]. And since this title is his by the right of redemption [1 *Cor* 6.20], to know the one Lord is to own and obey but one will [1 *Cor* 7.23]. Hence no true Christian can regard Christ as a mere man who attained a dubious kind of divinity, for he is the one Lord from whom all other lordship is derived and to whom it is accountable [1 *Cor* 8.6]. It is this common confession which binds men together as nothing else can. 'Where there is "the same Lord" [*Rom* 10.12], Jews and Gentiles, black and white, rich and poor, great and small, are yoked together' (Foulkes).

5. one faith Because there is one Lord, there can be only one faith in him, one way of being saved by him. It therefore follows that this subjective trust in Christ, this believing in him, is exactly the same for all, whether Jew or Gentile. For there is no way to the Father save through him who is the way, the truth, and the life [*John* 14.6].

6. one baptism The one faith which unites the believer with one Lord is visibly confessed in one baptism [*Rom* 6.3; *Gal* 3.27]. Baptism, and not the Lord's Supper is mentioned, because this is the initiatory rite in which *all* are joined by one Spirit to the one body [cf 1 *Cor* 12.13]. The repeated 'all' of this verse shows that the gift of the Spirit is not reserved for a privileged minority in the church, but is bestowed upon every believer without distinction. In the New Testament it is only in connection with John's baptism that Spirit-baptism is contrasted with water-baptism [cf *Acts* 19.2, 3]. For in the experience of the early church the work of the Spirit in conversion and the gift of the Spirit in baptism were so closely associated that they were regarded as constituent parts of the same event. And this is why the apostles nowhere exhort believers to be baptized with the Spirit, though Paul directs them to 'be filled with the Spirit' [see comment on 5.18].

7: one God and Father of all, who is over all, and through all, and in all. The final item in the series is a triad which crowns the two previous triads. As their Creator, God is the Father of all men, but this 'all' speaks of his special relation to all the sons of faith, who are united to him by the double tie of creation and redemption. 'The apostle does not refer to the dominion of God over the universe, or to his providential agency throughout all nature. Neither is the reference to his dominion over rational creatures or over mankind. It is the relation of God to the church, of which the whole passage treats. God as Father is over all its members, through them all and in them all. The church is a habitation of God through the Spirit. It is his temple in which he dwells and which is pervaded in all its parts by his presence ... This is the climax. To be filled with God; to be pervaded by his presence, and controlled by him, is to attain the summit of all created excellence, blessedness and glory' (Charles Hodge).

*V*7: **But unto each one of us was the grace given according to the measure of the gift of Christ.**

But the unity of the body does not mean that its members are characterized by a drab uniformity, for each was given by the exalted Christ in sovereign wisdom that measure of grace which manifests itself in his particular gift [*v* 16; cf 1 *Cor* 12.4ff]. And as this grace 'is not bestowed upon us to diffuse and lose itself in our separate individualities' (Findlay), every member must recognize that this distribution of diverse gifts is made for 'the building up of the body of Christ' [*v* 12]. Paul thus establishes three facts: (1) Because 'the grace' is given to *each one*, 'nobody in the church need feel that he is of no use or without a task'; (2) because it is a *divine gift* it is not a thing the Christian can grasp by himself; (3) this grace *is different* in various members, 'All have not gifts of equal size and nature, but the gift is under all conditions such as Christ has decided' (Hanson).

*V*8: **Wherefore he saith,**
> **When he ascended on high,**
> **he led captivity captive,**
> **And gave gifts unto men.**

Wherefore he saith, '*Who* says it (comp 5.14) is obvious of itself, namely, *God*, whose word the Scripture is' (Meyer).

When he ascended on high, *Psalm* 68.16 celebrates the arrival of the ark of the Lord in Jerusalem, whose dignity is not derived from its physical height, but from its spiritual elevation as God's designated dwelling-place. The verse quoted shows that it is after the conquest of the enemy's citadel that Jehovah 'ascends' the earthly sanctuary of Mount Zion to share the spoils of victory with his people [*Ps* 68.18]. But Paul sees that these words have found a still higher fulfilment in Christ's triumphant ascension to the seat of universal sovereignty in heaven, from whence he dispenses the gifts of his grace upon the church [*v* 7].

he led captivity captive, The captives in the Victor's train are not the redeemed, but the vanquished powers of evil. For at the cross 'captivity' itself was taken captive, and the hellish rule of these hostile powers over mankind was broken [*Col* 2.15; *Heb* 2.14; cf *Mark* 3.27].

And gave gifts unto men. It is in order to set forth the true Messianic application of this passage that Paul here diverges from both the Septuagint and the Hebrew text which read: 'received gifts for (among) men.' But the difference is more apparent than real,[1] for 'what Christ receives mediatorially he receives to bestow on his people, as Peter reminded his hearers on the day of Pentecost [*Acts* 2.33]. They are blessed with all spiritual endowments in and through him. N.T. quotations of O.T. passages are also authoritative interpretations of the significance of these passages. The Spirit of God knows his own letter-press better than the most lynx-eyed modern critic, so often "all eyes and no sight" ' (Simpson).

*V*9: (Now this, He ascended, what is it but that he also descended into the lower parts of the earth?

---

1. It is worth noting with Derek Kidner that this change 'summarizes rather than contradicts the psalm, whose next concern is with the blessings God dispenses [19ff, 35]' [*Psalms 1–72*, p. 242].

Now, the word 'ascended' implies that he also descended to the lowest level, down to the very earth. (NEB) As this ascension was the return of the One whose proper abode is heaven [cf *John* 3.13 NEB: 'whose home is in heaven'], it must also imply his previous descent to the earth, a descent in which he plumbed the lowest depth of humiliation for the sake of those he came to save. Thus we have here a pregnant reference to the same sequence which is fully described in *Phil* 2.6–11. 'Now *this* ascension whereby he, as Victor over Satan, sin, and death, re-entered heaven in the full merits of his atoning sacrifice would never have been possible had he not first descended from the glories of heaven to earth's shame and suffering' (Hendriksen).

*V*10: **He that descended is the same also that ascended far above all the heavens, that he might fill all things.)**

He who descended is no other than he who ascended far above all heavens, so that he might fill the universe.

(NEB) There is no reference here to a diffused and ubiquitous physical presence, but to a 'pervading and energizing omnipresence' (Ellicott). Paul is showing that the object of Christ's exaltation to the highest place that heaven affords 'was that he might enter into regal relation with the whole world and in that position and prerogative bestow his gifts as he willed and as they were needed. He was exalted in order that he might take kingly sway, fill the universe with his activity as its Sovereign and Governor, and his church with his presence as its Head, and provide his people with all needful grace and gifts' (Salmond) [*v* 11; cf 1.23].

*V*11: **And he gave some *to be* apostles; and some, prophets; and some, evangelists; and some, pastors and teachers;**

[87]

Among the gifts bestowed upon the church by the ascended Christ ('he' is emphatic), Paul here mentions in order of importance the *persons* whom he gave to serve the church at large as apostles, prophets, and evangelists, while those who have the task of pastor and teacher are evidently the resident overseers of local congregations. In stating that such men are *Christ's gift* Paul doubtless intends to evoke the *church's gratitude*. 'That we have ministers of the gospel is his gift; that they excel in necessary gifts is his gift; that they execute the trust committed to them, is likewise his gift' (Calvin).

1. **apostles** Here, as in 2.20, the word is used in the highest sense. 'The distinguishing features of an apostle were, a commission directly from Christ: being a witness of the resurrection: special inspiration: supreme authority: accrediting by miracles: unlimited commission to preach and to found churches' (Vincent).

2. **prophets** These were also extraordinarily endowed, 'not only in the more special sense [as Agabus, *Acts* 11.28], but in the more general one of preachers and expounders, who spoke under the immediate impulse and influence of the Holy Spirit, and were thus to be distinguished from the teachers' (Ellicott) [cf 2.20].

3. **evangelists** Of lower rank than the apostles under whom they worked, these men were itinerant preachers whose task was to spread the gospel in new places, as did Philip in Samaria and Caesarea [*Acts* 8.5ff].

4. **pastors and teachers** The construction here shows that the ministers of particular churches are assigned the dual function of guiding and feeding the flock over which they have been set [*Acts* 20.28]. 'No man is fit to be a pastor who cannot also teach, and the teacher needs the knowledge which pastoral experience gives' (Vincent).

*V*12: **for the perfecting of the saints, unto the work of ministering, unto the building up of the body of Christ:**

to equip God's people for work in his service, to the building up of the body of Christ. (NEB) As the NEB's omission of the first comma shows, the purpose for which Christ gave *these men* is that *all* God's people should be perfectly fitted for the particular service that each is to contribute to the building up of the body of Christ. In other words, Christ has appointed the ministry of the Word as the means by which all members of the church are equipped for Christian service in the world [cf 4.25–32; 5.21–6.9]. Thus Christ gave men to be the servants of the Word, so that through their ministry his Body might be built up. 'From this it is plain that those who neglect this means and yet hope to become perfect in Christ are mad. Such are the fanatics, who invent secret revelations of the Spirit for themselves, and the proud, who think that for them the private reading of the Scriptures is enough, and that they have no need of the common ministry of the church' (Calvin).

*V*13: **till we all attain unto the unity of the faith, and of the knowledge of the Son of God, unto a full-grown man, unto the measure of the stature of the fulness of Christ:**

till we all attain unto the unity, Since this 'all' is the totality of the redeemed, it is clear that the purpose for which Christ gave the means of grace will be achieved only when the whole church has reached its appointed goal. And this will be attained 'when the members of the church have all come to their proper unity and maturity in their Head' (Salmond).

of the faith, and of the knowledge of the Son of God, This 'unity of the faith' is something more than a common assent to the objective truth of the gospel; it is that living unity among believers which is produced by their shared *experience* of 'the knowledge of the Son of God'. Paul uses this title here to bring out the essential and eternal dignity of the One with whom believers are thus united. They are already *individually* united with the Son of God [*Gal* 2.20], but they must constantly strive to realize their *corporate* unity in him, even though they know that its consummation belongs to the state of glory [cf 5.27].

unto a full-grown man, unto the measure of the stature of the fulness of Christ: Paul envisages the unity of the church in its final form by likening it to a 'full-grown' man, whose 'stature' corresponds to the 'full measure' of Christ. 'This perfect form is achieved when all who are appointed to it by the divine plan of salvation belong to the church. The emphasis is on the words *we all* [*v* 13a]. The church, which is the body of Christ, represents in its perfected form the *fulness* of Christ' (J. Schneider, *TDNT*, Vol. II, p. 943).

*V*14: **that we may be no longer children, tossed to and fro and carried about with every wind of doctrine, by**

the sleight of men, in craftiness, after the wiles of error; In the climax of the previous verse Paul set forth the ultimate goal of Christian growth, and he now states both negatively [*v* 14] and positively [*vv* 15, 16] how that great end is to be attained. For Christ gave us the ministry of the Word [*vv* 11, 12], so that we may be no longer like naïve children who are easily led astray from the truth. Paul's warning against spiritual immaturity is continued in a nautical image; he expects his readers to have such a firm grasp of the gospel that they will not be tossed about by the waves and winds of false doctrine, which are already unsettling their fellow-believers in nearby Colosse [cf *Col* 2.8].

[90]

The second half of the verse shows that Paul cannot speak of the dangers of false teaching without also describing the devious arts of those who propagate it. First, he uses the word 'sleight', which literally means 'dice-playing', to expose the trickery which underlies their plausible pretensions. And secondly, in drawing attention to their craftiness 'in deceitful *scheming*' (Arndt-Gingrich), he seems to suggest by his repetition of the word in 6.11 ('the *wiles* of the devil') that they owe this capacity to lead men into error to their real master [cf. *John* 8.44].

*V*15: **but speaking truth in love, may grow up in all things into him, who is the head,** *even* **Christ;**
*V*16: **from whom all the body fitly framed and knit together through that which every joint supplieth, according to the working in** *due* **measure of each several part, maketh the increase of the body unto the building up of itself in love.**

but maintaining the truth in love (J. Armitage Robinson). It is preferable to adopt this rendering because Paul is here contrasting the truth with error [*v* 14]. But just as error and deceit always go together, so truth and love are inseparably conjoined 'as the twin conditions of growth' (J. Armitage Robinson). 'Truth without love lacks its proper environment and loses its persuasive power; love without truth forfeits its identity, degenerating into maudlin sentiment without solidity, feeling without principle' (R. M. McCheyne).

may grow up in all things into him, It is simpler to refer this back to the 'full-grown' man of verse 13 than to link it with the next phrase, which involves the difficulty of explaining how we can grow into Christ as the Head. When we thus take the words as complete in themselves, they point to a process of growth in which the members are to reach perfect conformity with Christ. According to Paul, individual development is subordinated to the growth of the whole body, and this means that Christ's gifts are imparted not for private edification, but so that each member may be able to make his distinctive contribution to the building up of Christ's body [cf 1 *Cor* 12].

who is the head, *even* Christ, It is because the significance of Christ cannot be contained within one metaphor that Paul now advances to the thought of the Head. For though Christ is the whole body because all the members are in him [*John* 15.1; *Rom* 12.5; 1 *Cor* 12.12], he is far more than the sum total of his members! He is also the Head of the body, 'which stands over against him no matter how much it is also one with him' (E. Schweizer, *TDNT*, Vol. VII, p. 1080).

from whom the whole body, joined and knit together by every joint with which it is supplied, (RSV) It is from Christ the Head that the whole body derives its life, nourishment, and well-ordered growth [cf *Col* 2.19]. And the fact that Paul assigns the key rôle in this process to 'every joint' leads R. P. Martin to suggest an identification with Christ's gift of the ministry [*v* 11], through which the Word of his grace reaches all the members ('each several part').

according to the proportionate working of each several part, (Abbott). Thus the vertical descent of Christ's grace finds its expression in the horizontal harmony of the members. Paul sees this spiritual truth illustrated in the growth of a healthy body in which there are no disproportionate developments. For each part receives that measure of grace which determines its proper contribution to the functioning of the whole body.

maketh the increase of the body unto the building up of itself in love. Paul's remarkable conclusion is that the church thus acquires the power to grow and build *itself* up, though he is careful to add that this is only achieved in caring love. This means that there is no room in the church for a selfish individualism that neglects the need to serve its fellow-members. 'As every member in a body has a task to fulfil, and exists for the sake of the body as a whole. so has every Christian a function in the church, however different it may be, and only if each one's gift is placed in the service of the whole, i.e. if *love* is allowed to be the superior principle, is the unity and growth of the church promoted' (Hanson).

*V*17: **This I say therefore, and testify in the Lord, that ye no longer walk as the Gentiles also walk, in the vanity of their mind,**

Having shown the readers the glory of the body to which they belong, Paul is at last ready to enforce the consequences of that union in terms of everyday conduct [thus resuming the exhortation begun at *v* 1]. They must not mistake this for mere human advice, for he speaks with apostolic authority, 'identifying himself with Christ and giving the exhortation as one made by Christ himself' (Salmond).

that ye no longer walk as indeed the Gentiles walk, in the vanity of their mind, (Bruce). As befits those who are members of 'the Israel of God' [*Gal* 6.16], they must no longer live as they once did [2.12] and as the unenlightened heathen still do. Paul's diagnosis of the evils of paganism is intended to put them on their guard against any relapse into what were now alien patterns of thought and behaviour. First he focuses attention upon the darkening effects of sin upon the mind. The Gentiles led frustrated, fruitless lives because their minds were 'fixed on futile things' (Arndt-Gingrich). With this one

word Paul exhibits the folly of the ancient world's empty re-
liance upon its own wisdom to find the meaning of life. Idolatry was the root cause of such vanity of mind [Rom 1.21], for
all who forsake the living God inevitably worship objects
which are void of value, and thus condemn themselves to a
purposeless existence.

*V*18: **being darkened in their understanding, alienated
from the life of God, because of the ignorance that is in
them, because of the hardening of their heart;**

being darkened in their understanding, The heathen pur-
sue this futile course because their understanding is in a state
of darkness. The retina of reason has been obscured by sin o
that the light of revelation makes no impression upon it. Yet
they consider this culpable condition of darkness to be normal
and proudly claim the ability to see [*Matt* 6.23; *Rom* 1.19–22].
'Many a present-day "scientist" claims to know, but knows
nothing as he ought to know it' (Lenski).

being . . . alienated from the life of God, This is co-or-
dinate with the previous clause and shows that the darkening of
the understanding necessarily involves a state of alienation from
God, who is the sole source of spiritual life [*John* 17.3; 1 *John*
5.11]. It is evident that such an estrangement must have the
direst consequences, for to be thus deprived of the highest
blessedness [2.12] also entails death in trespasses and sins [2.1].

because of the ignorance that is in them, Paul is not content to say that the miserable state of the heathen was due to
their ignorance; he traces it to the ignorance 'that is in them',
which suggests that it belongs to their very nature. 'It is not
an acquired ignorance that is due to absence of light and in-
formation; it is an original ignorance that is in them from the
start, the ignorance of inborn sin' (Lenski).

because of the petrifaction of their heart, (Lenski) This is the ultimate cause of their alienation. That they have no feeling for God is due to the rock-like hardness of their heart. 'This is what is wrong with the natural man; yes, he is blind and ignorant, but worse, his heart is stone [compare *Ezek* 11.19]' (Lenski). What then but divine omnipotence can suffice to change it?

*V*19: **who being past feeling gave themselves up to lasciviousness, to work all uncleanness with greediness.**

Paul now states the ethical consequences of this religious alienation. The inner petrifacation of the heathen was outwardly registered in their callous conduct. Impiety and impurity always go hand in hand, but those who make this terrible surrender to uncleanness may not complain when God justly confirms them in their vile choice [cf *Rom* 1.24]. 'With greediness' denotes the reckless rapacity that breaks through all restraints and violates all rights in its unlawful quest for satisfaction in *uncleanness*! History vouches for the accuracy of this frightful description of the shameless debauchery in which the Gentile world was sunk.

*V*20: **But ye did not so learn Christ;**

'But' is in emphatic contrast, as Paul reminds his believing readers that they did not (in their conversion: aorist tense) so learn Christ. This makes it clear that becoming a Christian involves more than the learning of a doctrine. It is nothing less than the learning of Christ as Saviour and Lord, which means that authentic discipleship includes the dynamic that enables a man to lead a disciplined life [cf *Matt* 11.28-30]. It is therefore as Christ's disciples that they have learned to renounce the way of darkness and death and to follow his way of light and life. In the next four verses the full consequences of this learning of Christ are gratefully recalled [*vv* 21–24]. 'Usually we learn subjects, not persons; but the Christian's choicest lesson-book is his loveworthy Lord. Instruction about him falls short of the mark; personal intimacy is requisite to rivet the bond of union with the Saviour' (Simpson).

*V*21: **if so be that ye heard him, and were taught in him, even as truth is in Jesus:**

'If so be' implies no doubt but takes it as certain that they both heard Christ and were taught in union with him. 'Christ himself is the Christians' Teacher, even if the teaching is given through the lips of his followers; to receive the teaching is in the truest sense to hear him' (Bruce) [cf *Acts* 1.1].

even as truth is in Jesus: In using the name of Jesus by itself [only here in this Epistle, cf *Phil* 2.10], Paul draws attention to the Incarnate Saviour as the very embodiment of truth. It is because Jesus *is* the truth in all its saving fulness that we can be said to 'learn him' [*John* 14.6].

*V*22: **that ye put away, as concerning your former manner of life, the old man, that waxeth corrupt after the lusts of deceit;**
*V*23: **and that ye be renewed in the spirit of your mind,**
*V*24: **and put on the new man, that after God hath been created in righteousness and holiness of truth.**

so that ye have put off, according to the former manner of life, the old man who is corrupted according to the lusts of deceit, (Murray).[1] It is not in harmony with Paul's

---

1. The translation followed in *vv* 22–24 is that given by John Murray in his *Principles of Conduct*, pp. 214–215, to which the interested reader is referred for its grammatical justification.

teaching elsewhere to interpret this passage in terms of an exhortation. It rather sets forth the *result* of the Ephesians' learning of Christ: they have put off the old man and have put on the new man! That such a decisive change is in view here, and that it provides the *basis* of the ensuing exhortation [*vv* 25–32], is apparent from the parallel passage in *Col* 3.9, 10, where believers are admonished, 'Lie not to one another', precisely because they 'have put off the old man with his doings'. Moreover, in *Rom* 6.6 we have the conclusive statement that 'our old man was crucified with him', from which it is clear that the old man is neither ailing nor dying, but dead and gone forever! Finally, we must reflect upon the implications of Paul's characterization of the old man, who has his pattern in 'the former manner of life' [as described in *vv* 17–19] and 'is corrupt according to the lusts of deceit'. The contrast Paul draws with the words, 'But ye did not so learn Christ', shows that he does not think of believers as answering to such a description! [cf *v* 24].

and are being renewed in the spirit of your mind, (Murray). The consequence of their having put off the old man is that they are being progressively renewed in the spirit of their mind. Although the Spirit is the unnamed agent behind this 'being renewed', what is stressed here is that it is by the transformation of the governing spirit of the mind that this renewal is taking place [cf *Rom* 8.16 for this distinction between the Holy Spirit and the human spirit]. Regeneration adds nothing to the properties and processes of the mind as a functioning organism, but the mind's character or prevailing bent is so entirely changed by this renewing of its motivating spirit that the result can only be described as a new creation.

and have put on the new man who after God has been created in righteousness and holiness of the truth. (Murray). The subject of this process of renewal is here identified with the new man they became when they put on Christ [*Gal* 3.27]. The new man has been created after the likeness of God [*Gen* 1.27] in that righteousness and holiness which are born of the truth of the gospel [1 *Pet* 1.23]. And it is because such a *definitive breach* with the old life has been made that believers are urged to bring their behaviour into conformity with the new identity which is theirs in Christ [2.10; 2 *Cor* 5.17]. It is this objective sanctification already possessed in Christ [1 *Cor* 1.30] that lays upon them the solemn obligation to live a righteous and holy life [1 *Pet* 1.16]. For clearly it is monstrous for those who are now in union with Christ to present again their 'members unto sin as instruments of un-righteousness' [*Rom* 6.13; cf 1 *Cor* 6.15ff]. John Murray sums up his illuminating discussion of these verses by drawing this important conclusion: 'The believer is a new man, a new creation, but he is a new man not yet made perfect. Sin dwells in him still, and he still commits sin. He is necessarily the subject of progressive renewal ... But this *progressive* renewal is not represented as the putting off of the old man and the putting on of the new ... It does mean the mortification of the deeds of the flesh and of all sin in heart and life. But it is the renewal of the "new man" unto the attainment of that glory for which he is destined, conformity to the image of God's Son' (*Principles of Conduct*, p. 219).

*V*25: **Wherefore, putting away falsehood, speak ye truth each one with his neighbour; for we are members one of another.**

Wherefore having put off then once for all falsehood in its every form, speak ye truth each one with his neighbour: (Salmond). Paul wishes believers to understand why they must speak the truth; it is because they finished with all falsehood when they put off the old man [v 22]. The genesis of all sin lay in the acceptance of the devil's lie, and this outright rejection of God's Word made 'truth' a relative concept for the old man, whose whole life was lived under the dominion of deceit. But it is as those who have for ever renounced all duplicity that believers must continually speak the truth ['in love', vv 15, 16] to one another [Zech 8.16].

for we are members one of another. Lying is never beneficial, but always injurious in its effects. Hence it would be in the highest degree unnatural for fellow-members of the same body to harm one another in this way [Rom 12.5]. As Chrysostom strikingly remarks, 'If the eye sees a serpent, does it deceive the foot? if the tongue tastes what is bitter, does it deceive the stomach?'

V26: **Be ye angry, and sin not; let not the sun go down upon your wrath:**
V27: **neither give place to the devil.**

Be angry, but do not sin: (Arndt-Gingrich). A quotation of Ps 4.4 according to the Septuagint. 'The easiest charge under the hardest condition that can be. Anger is a tender virtue, and must be warily managed. He that will be angry and not sin, let him be angry at nothing but sin' (Trapp) [cf Mark 3.5].

let not the sun go down upon your wrath: Yet even righteous anger may not be cherished [v 31], but must be dismissed before the day is over. It seems likely that Paul's imagery here was influenced by the second part of Ps 4.4: 'commune with your own heart upon your bed, and be still'. It is interesting to compare this verse with James 1.19 as they place a double restraint upon this dangerous emotion: Christians are not only to be *slow* to anger but also *quick* to overcome it! (cf G. Stählin, *TDNT*, Vol. V, p. 421).

and give no opportunity to the devil. (RSV) Or '*do not give the devil a chance* to exert his influence' (Arndt-Gingrich). 'We are neither to cherish anger, nor are we to allow Satan to take advantage of our being angry. Anger when cherished gives the Tempter great power over us, as it furnishes a motive to yield to his evil suggestions' (Charles Hodge).

*V*28: **Let him that stole steal no more; but rather let him labour, working with his hands the thing that is good, that he may have thereof to give to him that hath need.**

With Paul the demand to desist from vice is always an occasion for enjoining the practice of the opposite virtue. So here the condemnation of what is wrongly gained by stealing leads to the positive teaching that the believer may not eat the bread of idleness but is to earn an honourable living [2 *Thess* 3.6–12]. Hence not only must the former thief no longer steal; he must now use his hands to engage in honest toil so that he may have the means to help his needy brother [*Gal* 6.10]. 'The Christian philosophy of labour is thus lifted far above the thought of what is right or fair in the economic field; it is lifted to the place where there is no room for selfishness or the motive of personal profit at all. Giving becomes the motive for getting' (Foulkes).

*V*29: **Let no corrupt speech proceed out of your mouth, but such as is good for edifying as the need may be, that it may give grace to them that hear.**

No bad language is to escape the lips of believers, who are to produce evidence of the reality of a cleansed heart by the

purity of their speech [*Luke* 6.45]. Shunning the defiling utterance that destroys, they are to speak words that will build
up, wisely chosen to suit the occasion so that they may be the
means of blessing those who hear them. 'Even words good in
themselves must be introduced seasonably, lest they prove injurious instead of useful. Not vague generalities, which would
suit a thousand other cases equally well or ill: our words
should be as nails fastened in a sure place, words suiting the
present time and the present person' (Fausset).

*V*30: **And grieve not the Holy Spirit of God, in whom
ye were sealed unto the day of redemption.**

'And' indicates that this exhortation is closely connected with
the preceding injunction. Since the Spirit specially claims to
control the speech of believers [5.18f] he is grieved when his
sanctifying work in them is hindered by their abuse of the
very gift which should further it. And to make them realize
the enormity of the offence, Paul writes, the *Holy* Spirit *of
God*. 'It is not an influence that these sacrileges stifle, but a
sacred Person they repel' (Simpson). At first sight it is perhaps
surprising that Paul should choose to base his appeal for
obedience upon the *security* of believers [1.13, 14]. 'Men may
think that a stronger appeal might be based on fear lest we
fall from the Spirit's keeping; as if Paul should rather have
said, Because you can be kept only by the Spirit, beware lest
you grieve him away by sinning. But Paul's actual appeal is
not to fear but to gratitude. Because you have been sealed by
the Spirit unto the day of redemption, see to it that you do
not grieve, bring pain or sorrow to this Spirit, who has done
so much for you' (B. B. Warfield, *Faith and Life*, pp. 294–295).

*V*31: **Let all bitterness, and wrath, and anger, and clam-
our, and railing, be put away from you, with all malice:**

This terse but telling arrangement of terms is in itself a powerful dissuasive against any indulgence in such sins. Paul thus shows how one sin leads to another. For 'bitterness' nurses the hatred which finds expression in 'anger' and 'wrath', and these induce unbridled denunciation and violent cursing. *All* these together with *all* 'malice' – the frightful animus which inspires this evil speaking – 'are to be put away in every kind and degree – in germ as well as maturity – without reserve and without compromise' (Eadie).

*V*32: **and be ye kind one to another, tenderhearted, forgiving each other, even as God also in Christ forgave you.**

Paul follows the negative with the positive. Believers must also show themselves to be of another spirit, always manifesting mutual kindness and tenderness of heart, and freely forgiving one another's faults and failings without grudging. This is not put forward as a counsel of perfection, but as the only practical norm for maintaining fellowship among those who have not yet been made perfect [*Matt* 18.21, 22]. The supreme motive for this waiving of the petty debts of our fellow-men is furnished by what God did in Christ to secure our discharge from the immense debt of sin. This we are to forgive 'even as' we have been forgiven [*Matt* 18.33]. 'Observe that the cross of Christ is the sole medium of gospel forgiveness. All pardons pass through Immanuel's hands. God's evangel exhibits a miracle of mercy that should ensure largeheartedness in its recipients; but that mercy is essentially *cruciform*' (Simpson).

CHAPTER FIVE

The apostle insists that believers must strive to be like God as the true children of their heavenly Father. They must be distinguished by the purity of their lives in contrast to the immorality of those who will incur God's wrath. They must not only refuse to have fellowship with such people but must expose the real nature of their evil deeds [vv 1–14]. He also directs them to walk wisely, to make good use of the time, and to understand the Lord's will for them. Instead of indulging in riotous revelry, they are to be filled with the Spirit, whose gracious presence is evidenced in the joyful thanksgiving and reverent worship which promotes the Christian grace of mutual submission [vv 15–21]. The mention of this general principle leads Paul to speak of the submission which wives owe to their husbands. This injunction is illustrated by Christ's relation to his church, which is compared to that of the husband to the wife. As the church is subject to Christ, so the wife should be subject to her husband. And just as Christ loved the church and gave himself up for it, so the husband should love his wife. The comparison not only ennobles the marriage relationship itself, but also provides Paul with the opportunity to expound his doctrine of the church: Christ is the Saviour of his body the church, which he cleansed by his sacrifice so that he might present it to himself without blemish. And he cares for it in the same way as a man nourishes his own flesh [vv 22–33].

V_I: **Be ye therefore imitators of God, as beloved children;**

*V*2: **and walk in love, even as Christ also loved you, and gave himself up for us, an offering and a sacrifice to God for an odour of a sweet smell.**

Although these verses are usually regarded as rounding off the preceding exhortation, it is preferable to understand them as providing the foundation of the following admonition against filthiness [*vv* 3–14]. Having shown how believers should treat one another, Paul is now ready to instruct them on their behaviour in a world which is full of temptations for the unwary [*vv* 6, 7]. But before giving them detailed counsel, he wants them to grasp the fact that they cannot remain distinct from the world unless they cherish their new identity, and keep in mind the cost of their deliverance from its evil ways [*Gal* 1.4]. Hence the bold call to become 'imitators of God, as beloved children'. As it is natural for children to imitate their parents, so the children of grace must always seek to reflect the perfections of their heavenly Father [cf 1 *Pet* 1.14–16]. 'We can be only "imitators", but we are to be that always' (Lenski).

and walk in love, even as Christ also loved you, This 'imitation' of God is to be shown in a life of love, which finds its motive and model in Christ's self-giving love. Obviously we cannot copy God in his creative or redemptive work, but our experience of his love towards us in Christ must lead us to walk before him in love – an exclusive relationship which bars us from all lust [*vv* 3–7].

and gave himself up for us, an offering and a sacrifice to God What Paul briefly indicates here is fully expounded in Hebrews, where it is demonstrated that Christ's surrender to the death of the cross on our behalf was in fact the priestly offering of himself to God as the complete sacrifice for sin [cf *Heb* 9.14]. In one great transaction our Mediator then ful-

filled all that was signified by the typical ceremonies prescribed under the law [cf *Heb* 10.1–10].

for an odour of a sweet smell. In words that recall *Gen* 8.21
Paul expresses the acceptability of this sacrifice to God. We
who have been reconciled to God by the sweet fragrance of
Christ's sacrifice can never return to a life that reeks with the
vile stench of sin.

V3: **But fornication, and all uncleanness, or covetousness, let it not even be named among you, as becometh
saints;**

**But immorality and impurity of any kind, or greed, let
it not even be mentioned among you,** (Hendriksen). This
rigorous demand to shun every form of moral laxity is an
emphatic condemnation of a course of living which was all
but universal in the ancient Gentile world. Paul insists that
the Christian community must be so sharply distinguished
from the surrounding corruption that its members should be
above even the suspicion of indulging in such degrading
practices. In view of the present context, 'greed' [cf 4.19] is
more likely to refer to uncontrolled sexual desire than to
avarice. What the world calls romantic love is really the ob-
sessive lust that gratifies itself without regard to the injury
that is done to others. But Christians must cherish a higher
standard of living than this, [cf 1 *Thess* 4.6].

as becometh saints; 'The title "saints" makes prominent
their relation to God. The apostle thus employs a term that
brings out the peculiar unfitness of the slightest approach to
impurity on the part of those who profess to be related to the
God of holiness [comp 1 *Cor* 6.15]' (Macpherson).

*V*4: **nor filthiness, nor foolish talking, or jesting, which are not befitting: but rather giving of thanks.**

Believers must also be on their guard against spreading the contagion of filthiness by sinful language. Hence Paul exhorts them to abstain from all foul, foolish, and facetious talk ['filthiness' is used here in the same sense as 'shameful speaking' in *Col* 3.8]. As Trench points out, 'foolish talking' means more than idle words; it is that 'talk of fools' which is foolishness and sin together. He further observes that 'jesting' is wit enlisted in the service of sin, and recalls the line of Plautus, the Roman comic poet, in which an old profligate boasts that his clever ribaldry is just what was to be expected of one who was born in Ephesus! Paul effectively condemns such sinful speech by mildly stating that it does not befit believers, who are rather to express their gratitude to God in words of thanksgiving. It is this that 'lifts us above the vileness of worldlings. Amid our Father's blessings with hearts and lips full of thanksgiving, these filthy vices will not even be named among us' (Lenski).

*V*5: **For this ye know of a surety, that no fornicator, nor unclean person, nor covetous man, who is an idolater, hath any inheritance in the kingdom of Christ and God.**

'If *pleonexia* is simply "covetousness", the question is, why should this, any more than fornication and impurity, be singled out to be called idolatry?' (Abbott). But this difficulty disappears if the word is given the wider meaning advocated in 4.19 and 5.3. Then we have a natural climax: 'For you are well aware of the fact that no immoral or impure person, or greedy man who is an idolater (because he makes sex his god!) has any inheritance in the (one) kingdom of Christ and God.' Although it is grammatically possible to regard Paul as here identifying Christ with God (as in *Titus* 2.13), such a reference would appear alien to the context. Nevertheless, we should not fail to note that the One who can be linked together with God under one definite article is no mere created being, but the very Son of God himself.

*V*6: **Let no man deceive you with empty words: for because of these things cometh the wrath of God upon the sons of disobedience.**

Let all believers be on their guard against being deceived by anyone who should try to excuse or even advocate the practice of these vices. For such 'empty words' are quite 'alien to the *solidity* of the immoveable *facts* that the body cannot sin without sin of the spirit; that body and spirit alike are concerned in eternal retribution; that the wrath of God is no figure of speech, and that his love cannot possibly modify his holiness' (Moule, *CB*). This wrath is the righteous reaction of God in manifesting his active displeasure against sin. There is a partial disclosure of God's wrath in the present experience of 'the sons of disobedience' [cf 2.2.], who live in wilful rebellion against his revealed will [*Rom* 1.18ff], though its final outpouring awaits the last day [*Rom* 2.5].

*V*7: **Be not ye therefore partakers with them;**

'Lest by infection of their sin ye come under infliction of their punishment' (Trapp). Rather they must stand entirely aloof from these workers of iniquity as befits those who have been called to share in a very different destiny [cf 3.6].

*V*8: **for ye were once darkness, but are now light in the Lord: walk as children of light**

It is only in terms of an absolute antithesis that Paul can adequately express the contrast between what his readers once were and what they are now [*vv* 8–14]. Formerly they were 'darkness', immured in a darkness that was all their own; now they are 'light', but this enlightenment is theirs only in the Lord. And they must so abide in him that no darkening by sin will prevent them from being the clean reflectors of this light to others [*Matt* 5.14].

walk as children of light Having been thus delivered from the dominion of darkness they are to evidence the reality of this blessed change by walking as children of light [cf *Col* 1.12f; 1 *John* 1.5–7]. This exhortation teaches us that light is never given for mere intellectual illumination, but always to promote practical obedience. Our daily conduct must make credible our confession of faith in Christ. For though man cannot look into the heart, he does closely observe the outward appearance we present to the world [cf 1 *Sam* 16.7].

*V*9: **(for the fruit of the light is in all goodness and righteousness and truth),**

The purpose of this parenthesis is to show what it means to walk as children of light. The moral fruit of the light is seen in every form of 'goodness and righteousness and truth', which are the opposite of all 'malice' [4.31], unrighteousness, and falsehood. The entire Christian ethic is summed up in the good, the right, and the true. As the light never changes, so this standard remains constant in every age. 'The only progress possible is to enter more deeply into these three. It is one of the lies of our time that we have progressed beyond them' (Lenski).

*V*10: **proving what is well-pleasing unto the Lord;**

Those who are bidden to 'walk as children of light' [*v* 8] will make it their constant aim to find out and follow that which 'is well-pleasing unto the Lord', i.e. Christ [cf *Rom* 12.2]. 'The believer is not to prove and discover what suits himself, but what pleases his divine Master. The one point of his ethical investigation is, Is it pleasing to the Lord, or in harmony with his law and example?' (Eadie).

*V*11: **and have no fellowship with the unfruitful works of darkness, but rather even reprove them;**
*V*12: **for the things which are done by them in secret it is a shame even to speak of.**
*V*13: **But all things when they are reproved are made manifest by the light: for everything that is made manifest is light.**

and have no fellowship with the unfruitful works of darkness, The incongruity of such an association is apparent, for 'what fellowship has light with darkness?' [2 *Cor* 6.14ff]. It is plainly absurd to expect 'the fruit of the light' [*v* 9] to flourish in the midst of darkness, that ethically sterile sphere whose only products are the barren works of death [cf *Rom* 6.21].

but rather expose them: for of the things which are done of them in secret it is a shame even to speak; (J. Armitage Robinson). Rather, since they 'are now light in the Lord' [*v* 8], they must let their light so shine forth that it shows up the real nature of those deeds of darkness which are too shameful even to mention. 'So the meaning is that the Christian, by a life so essentially different from those around him, rather than by reproof in speech, is to "expose" their sins' (Foulkes).

but all things when they are exposed by the light are made manifest; (J. Armitage Robinson). When the light of God breaks in to *expose* these works for what they are, this *conviction* of sin will lead men to forsake the darkness and turn to the light [as explained in *John* 3.20, 21].

for whatsoever is made manifest is light. (J. Armitage Robinson). This manifestation therefore leads to a transformation. For as the light of the gospel first disclosed and then dispelled the former darkness of Paul's readers [*v* 8], so they may now be used to bring the same enlightenment to their heathen neighbours. Thus, as F. F. Bruce helpfully paraphrases it, 'Whatever abandons the darkness and is made manifest by the light belongs henceforth to the light'.

*V*14: **Wherefore** *he* **saith, Awake, thou that sleepest, and arise from the dead, and Christ shall shine upon thee.**

Wherefore *he* **saith,** At first sight it is remarkable that the same phrase which introduced the words of Scripture [4.8] should be used here to introduce what appears to be part of a Christian hymn. But the difficulty disappears when we see that such snatches of sacred song only found a place in the written Word of God because they were first inspired by the Holy Spirit [cf *'spiritual'* songs', *v* 19]. The quotation is in the form of a metrical triplet:

> **Awake, O sleeper,**
> **From the grave arise.**
> **The light of Christ upon you shines.** (Martin)

The most likely setting of this exhortation is baptism, which was known in the later church as 'enlightenment'. As the congregation sang these lines, the convert would emerge from the water in the confidence that he had quit the grave of sin for a new life in Christ [cf *Rom* 6.4ff; *Col* 2.12]. 'Paul harks back to this experience as a reminder to his readers to fulfil now their baptismal profession by walking in Christ's light and by stirring themselves to active witness' (R. P. Martin, *NBC*).

*V*15: **Look therefore carefully how ye walk, not as unwise, but as wise;**

The word 'therefore' shows that the exhortation of verse 8 is here resumed. In view of the evils which surround them and their responsibility towards those who are without the light of saving truth [cf *Col* 4.5], believers are to give the most careful consideration to their conduct. They must walk 'not as unwise, but as wise'. The unsaved are the unwise who behave unwisely because they either follow a course of unthinking worldliness, or rely on that worldly wisdom which God has reduced to foolishness. But something better is to be expected of those whose wisdom has its root in the knowledge of God and its fruit in obedience to his will [cf *Ps* 111.10].

*V*16: **redeeming the time, because the days are evil.**

buying up the opportunity, (ASV margin) 'As wise merchants, trading for the most precious commodity, and taking their best opportunity. The common complaint is, We want time; but the truth is, we do not so much want it, as waste it' (Trapp). So believers must not take after the unwise who heedlessly fritter away their brief span, but are rather to buy up every opportunity that presents itself for the doing of God's will in the world.

because the days are evil. 'If these days so evil afforded any opportunities of doing good, it was all the more incumbent on Christians to win them and seize them. The very abundance of the evil was a powerful argument to redeem the time, and the apostle writing that letter in a prison was a living example of his own counsel' (Eadie)'

*V*17: **Wherefore be ye not foolish, but understand what the will of the Lord is.**

This amplifies the summons to walk wisely which was given in verse 15. If believers are to redeem the time they must not lapse into the senseless behaviour which belonged to their former state, and this can be avoided only if they clearly grasp what the will of the Lord is [cf *v* 10]. Thus in every situation the Christian's paramount concern must be to discern and do the will of Christ his *Lord*. 'Others may direct their minds to other questions such as: "What will bring me earthly gain, honour, pleasure, ease, etc.? What do others say, advise, do?" This is not only wrong, it is folly, senselessness. He is a fool who asks thus and determines his judgement and his life accordingly' (Lenski).

*V*18: **And be not drunken with wine, wherein is riot, but be filled with the Spirit;**

An outstanding example of such 'want of sense' is drunkenness [*v* 17], which Paul emphatically contrasts with the filling of the Spirit. 'Men are said to be filled with wine when completely under its influence; so they are said to be filled with the Spirit, when he controls all their thoughts, feelings, words, and actions' (Charles Hodge). But whereas a filling of wine results in debauchery and dissipation, the Spirit's fulness is manifested in the spiritual graces which are described in *vv* 19–21. In this masterly fashion the apostle combines a needful warning on the danger of over-indulgence in wine with the directive to receive the one safeguard against this temptation [cf on the sinful abuse of wine, *Rom* 13.13; 1 *Cor* 11.21; 1 *Tim* 3.8; *Titus* 2.3]. Thus instead of the riotous revelry of the tipler in his cups, there is to be the sensible enjoyment of the Spirit whose presence is always marked by the grace of 'self-control' [*Gal* 5.23].

Believers are here commanded to go on being filled with the Spirit, but are nowhere exhorted to be baptized (or sealed) with the Spirit because this blessing was conferred upon them in conversion [1 *Cor* 12.13; cf 1.13, 4.30]. The difference between the baptism and the fulness of the Spirit is illustrated by the state of the church at Corinth when Paul first wrote to the believers there. For though they had been baptized with the Holy Spirit, and were richly endowed with the gifts of the Spirit, they were not filled with the Spirit. And throughout the Epistle the apostle rebukes them for their unspiritual conduct in walking as men [compare for example *v* 21 with the behaviour reflected in 1 *Cor* 3.1-3; 11.20-22].

To be filled with the Spirit thus involves our submission to the control of the Spirit in every aspect of our lives. This is not an optional extra for the 'keen Christian', but a demand which is binding upon all believers. It means that we must avoid grieving or quenching the Spirit, and that we are to be always sensitive to his promptings. In short, there must be a continuous appropriation of the Spirit's fulness. Clearly this is not a once-for-all experience. For it is to the extent that this filling is known by Christians that the greater beauty of Christian living will be displayed in them [see comment on *vv* 19-21].

*V*19: **speaking one to another in psalms and hymns and spiritual songs, singing and making melody with your heart to the Lord;**
*V*20: **giving thanks always for all things in the name of our Lord Jesus Christ to God, even the Father;**
*V*21: **subjecting yourselves one to another in the fear of Christ.**

In these verses the present participles ('speaking', 'singing and making melody', 'giving thanks', and 'subjecting') depend on

[113]

the main verb of the previous verse ('be filled'), and thus describe the blessed consequences of the Holy Spirit's fulness.

speaking one to another in psalms and hymns and spiritual songs, As the parallel passage in *Col* 3.16 indicates, the fellowship of believers is founded upon their mutual submission to 'the word of Christ' whose reception is marked by the response of praise [cf the punctuation of RSV, NEB]. Hence this verse does not mean that believers receive instruction solely by means of song! The importance of singing in the worship of the early church is illustrated in a letter written by Pliny to the Emperor Trajan about AD 112. He reports that the Christians of his province gathered regularly on a fixed day before dawn to sing antiphonally 'a hymn to Christ as God'. It is doubtful whether these terms can be clearly distinguished. 'Psalms' may point to the Christian adoption of the Old Testament Psalter, but in 1 *Cor* 14.26 an ecstatically-inspired hymn is evidently in view. 'Hymns' were probably like the samples of Christian praise that seem to be embedded in the New Testament [cf *v* 14; *Phil* 2.6–11; *Col* 1.15–20; 1 *Tim* 3.16]. 'Spiritual songs' are so designated to show the source of their inspiration. However, if as some scholars think, 'spiritual' covers all three terms, then the richness of the early church's worship is expressly attributed to the prompting of the Holy Spirit.

singing and making melody with your heart to the Lord; '*With*', not 'in' your heart (as in AV), because the exhortation is not to silent, but to *heartfelt* worship ('with *all* your heart,' RSV). In congregational singing the outward expression of praise must not outrun the spirit of inward devotion. As the mouth sings the words, so the heart is to be lifted up to the Lord. For spiritual worship demands spiritual men [*John* 4.24].

giving thanks always for all things in the name of our Lord Jesus Christ to God, even the Father; Another mark of the fulness of the Spirit is a constant sense of thankfulness to God for 'all things' [cf *Rom* 8.28]. These 'sovereign dispensations are a matter of gratitude, not for murmuring ... The mixed yarn of life, woven in the loom of heaven by the Father of mercies, traces a perfect design for those "in Christ", and their thanksgivings should reascend to him through their mediatorial All-in-all' (Simpson).

subjecting yourselves one to another in the fear of Christ.
Finally, reverence for Christ must prompt believers to subject themselves to one another [cf *John* 13.1-17]. For unless personal pride is mortified it is impossible to maintain that mutual fellowship which is the fruit of Christian humility [1 *Pet* 5.5]. 'Humble submission is such an important part of Christian behaviour that the verb occurs 32 times in the New Testament. Not self-assertion but self-submission is the hall-mark of the Spirit-filled Christian ... We should submit to others right up to the point where our submission to them would mean disloyalty to Christ' (John Stott).

*V*22: **Wives, *be in subjection* unto your own husbands, as unto the Lord.**

The wives to their own husbands as to the Lord! (Lenski).
Beginning with marriage Paul now enjoins the kind of submission that is required in *particular* relationships [*vv* 22-23; 6.1-4, 5-9]. The thought is so closely connected with the previous verse that it has to supply the verb which this sentence lacks. In pagan society the inferiority of women and their lawful subjugation by men was taken for granted. The apostle here challenges 'this fact of life' with the teaching which transformed the status of women in every society that accepted it. He bids every Christian wife so to subject herself to her *own* husband (not all men) that she regards this voluntary (not enforced) submission as a *part* of her obedience

to Christ. 'The idea is that the will of God who arranged the marriage relation at creation is likewise the will of the Lord Christ for Christian wives' (Lenski).

*V*23: **For the husband is the head of the wife, as Christ also is the head of the church,** *being* **himself the saviour of the body.**

This advances the reason for such wifely subjection. It is found in the headship that makes man the ruling partner in the marriage relation, an arrangement not only established by creation but also endorsed in redemption. For Paul's astounding analogy likens a husband's headship over his wife to Christ's headship over the church [1.22]. Certainly no higher view of the marriage bond can be imagined than this sublime conception which makes *obedience* a matter of devotion, and *authority* an expression of love.

being **himself the saviour of the body.** 'i.e. Christ is the Saviour of his church, implying that so likewise the husband is given to the wife to be a saviour to her, in maintaining, protecting, and defending her; and therefore the wife, if she regard her own good, should not grudge to be subject to him' (Poole) [cf *vv* 29–30].

*V*24: **But as the church is subject to Christ, so** *let* **the wives also** *be* **to their husbands in everything.**

As the church gladly submits to the rule of Christ her head, even so wives should be subject to their husbands in everything pertaining to their legitimate authority *as husbands*: 'everything not contrary to God' (Fausset). Christian wives must understand that equality within the sphere of grace [*Gal* 3.28; 1 *Pet* 3.7] does not set aside the God-given order for marriage. 'In the state of sin the divine and blessed order is disturbed in two directions: wives seek to rule their husbands and refuse loving self-subjection; husbands tyrannize their wives often to the point of enslaving them. Endless woe results. Christianity restores the divine order with all its happiness' (Lenski).

*V*25: **Husbands, love your wives, even as Christ also loved the church, and gave himself up for it;**

Turning now to husbands, Paul tells them to love their wives with the same kind of self-giving love which Christ showed for the church when he gave himself up to the death of the cross. In *Gal* 2.20 the apostle uses the same verbs to confess his own interest in Christ's death, whereas here the whole church is viewed as a collective person: the Bride to whom the heavenly Bridegroom betrothed himself in this costly covenant of love [cf *John* 3.29]. This remarkable image has its roots in the Old Testament where Jehovah's covenant with Israel is described in terms of the marriage relationship [*Hosea* 2.16; *Is* 54.5]. The rabbis traced this union back to the covenant at Sinai, where the law became the marriage contract, and Moses led the bride to God. The gospel sequel shows that the age of law has given place to the reign of grace, for the church is the Bride who is saved and sanctified by the Bridegroom's own blood [*Acts* 20.28], and Paul sees himself as taking over the rôle of Moses in leading the bride to her husband [2 *Cor* 11.2].

'The church's obedience to Christ, which is the wife's model for her duty to her husband, may fall short of what it should be; there are no shortcomings about the love of Christ for his church, which is here prescribed as the model for the Christian husband's love for his wife. By setting this highest of standards for the husband's treatment of his wife, Paul goes to the limit in safeguarding the wife's dignity and welfare' (F. F. Bruce).

*V*26: **that he might sanctify it, having cleansed it by the washing of water with the word,**

that he might sanctify it, cleansing it by the washing of the water with (the) word, The immediate purpose for which Christ gave himself up was that he might sanctify and cleanse the church. The verbs are coincident in time, so that the aorist participle 'cleansing' expresses the way in which this sanctification was secured. Paul speaks of an objective accomplishment, and not of a subjective process. For in its most fundamental sense sanctification 'is not something that is worked up, but something that is rather sent down ... Holiness is not so much acquired as conceded ... it is less an activity than a status' (J. K. S. Reid, *A Theological Word Book of the Bible*, p. 217). Thus in verses 25–27 our attention is directed to the action of Christ; nothing is said of the activity of the church because this Bride provides her Husband with no dowry but receives everything from his nail-pierced hands [cf *Heb* 13.12].

'The washing of the water' evidently refers to baptism, but it is unique in that it speaks of the baptism of the church rather than of individuals. The salvation that is signified by baptism is conferred upon all the elect in connection with the word which the Spirit uses as his sword [6.17]. This 'word' is not a baptismal confession or formula, an idea which is in any case at variance with the corporate image used here; but the whole gospel, the preached message of salvation [cf. *Rom* 10.8a].

*V*27: **that he might present the church to himself a glorious *church*, not having spot or wrinkle or any such thing; but that it should be holy and without blemish.**

that he might himself present to himself the church, glorious, (Salmond). This states the ultimate purpose of

[118]

Christ's sacrifice [cf *Col* 1.22; *Rev* 19.7, 21.2]. 'The thought is of the heavenly Bridegroom welcoming the glorified Bride at the Marriage Feast hereafter. True, she is now "his Spouse and his Body"; but the manifestation then will be such as to be, in a sense, the Marriage as the sequel to the Betrothal. The words "present to himself" suggest that the Bride is not only to be welcomed then by her Lord, but welcomed as owing all her glory to his work, and as being now absolutely his own' (Moule, *CB*).

not having spot or wrinkle or any such thing; but that it should be holy and without blemish. Here the future glory of the church is first figuratively set forth in negative terms, and then literally expressed by the corresponding positive terms. At that great day Christ's *bride* shall be manifested in all the flawless beauty of unfading perfection, and this consummation of the *church* is the fulfilment of 'the original purpose of election formed before the foundation of the world' (Charles Hodge) [cf 1.4; *Jude* 24].

*V*28: **Even so ought husbands also to love their own wives as their own bodies. He that loveth his own wife loveth himself:**

Since Paul is a preacher of the gospel rather than a teacher of ethics, the response he asks for always assumes the reception of grace. So here it is Christ's love for the church that provides the pattern for the husband's love of his wife. Consequently 'ought' expresses not moral obligation, but spiritual indebtedness. It is because this word indicates the response to be expected from an experience of salvation, that such apostolic injunctions never 'lead into externally imposed legalism' (F. Hauck, *TDNT*, Vol. V, p. 564). In thus exhorting husbands to love their wives 'as their own bodies', Paul already seems to have in mind the words of *Gen* 2.24 [cf *v* 31].

He that loveth his own wife loveth himself: Paul follows the plural with the singular to bring the point home to every individual husband. As husband and wife share the same life whatever 'is done to one is done to both. This is not an appeal to the selfish principle of self-love, but the laying down of the law of community of interests' (Macpherson).

*V*29: **for no man ever hated his own flesh; but nourisheth and cherisheth it, even as Christ also the church;** *V*30: **because we are members of his body.**

This teaches us that it is not only a man's *duty* to love his wife, but also entirely *natural* that he should do so. For no man in his right mind ever hates his own flesh, but rather feeds it and tenderly cares for its every need. So she who is 'one flesh' [*v* 31] with him may justly expect to receive the same attention that he lavishes upon himself. In demanding the *God-given* rights of women in a world which generally regarded them as mere chattels, Paul is revealed as something more than the woman-hater his detractors allege him to be! It may also be noted that the passage offers cold comfort to those who wish to make their ascent to God by climbing the ladder of asceticism, for clearly only a fanatic hates his own flesh [cf *Col* 2.23].

even as Christ also the church; because we are members of his body. Once again Christ's example in caring for the church's every need is invoked as the pattern upon which the husband's behaviour towards his wife is to be modelled. This Christ does because we are members of his body [cf 4.7ff]. 'We are veritable parts of that body of which he is head, and this is the reason why he nourishes and cherishes the church' (Salmond).

*V*31: **For this cause shall a man leave his father and mother, and shall cleave to his wife; and the two shall become one flesh.**

As the ASV indicates, 'for this cause' belongs to *Gen* 2.24, which Paul now quotes to confirm the teaching of the previous verses [*vv* 28, 29a] and to exhibit the source of his imagery. This Scripture shows that the sanctity of the marriage bond is grounded in the intimacy of its union. It is because the two become one flesh that the violation of that bond is so great a sin [cf 1 *Cor* 6.16]. The significance of the verb order is succinctly noted by Derek Kidner: ' "leaving" before "cleaving"; marriage, nothing less, before intercourse. So this question, as well as divorce, was settled "from the beginning" [*Mark* 10.6ff]' (*Commentary on Genesis*, p. 66).

*V*32: **This mystery is great: but I speak in regard of Christ and of the church.**

Paul has quoted *Gen* 2.24 in its literal meaning and he returns to this sense in verse 33, but here he reveals its *mystic* or *hidden* significance (so Thayer, p. 420; cf NEB, 'It is a great truth that is hidden here'). Thus the apostle's extended analogy is based upon his inspired understanding of this Scripture, where he finds in the union of husband and wife a pre-figuration of the union of Christ and the church. For 'the meaning of that primary institution of human society, though proclaimed in dark words at the beginning of history, could not be truly known till its heavenly archetype was revealed, even the relation of Christ and the Ecclesia' (F. J. A. Hort). As the following verse shows, Paul's purpose is not speculative but practical: it is that this exalted conception may enrich and ennoble every Christian marriage.

*V*33: **Nevertheless do ye also severally love each one his own wife even as himself; and *let* the wife *see* that she fear her husband.**

Nevertheless 'Howbeit – not to dwell on this matter of Christ and the church, but to return to what I am treating of – .' (Abbott);

do ye also severally love each one his own wife even as himself; The 'also' is important for it alludes to the example of Christ, and means 'in you also, as in Christ, *love* is to be fulfilled'. Consequently the authority of the husband must be exercised in love. *Every* husband is *always* to love his *own wife* as being part and parcel of *himself.*

and let the wife see that she respects her husband. (RSV) It is important to understand that Paul's prescription for the ideal marriage is based upon the Christ-church relationship. Wives must be subject to their husbands because the church is under the control of Christ. Hence he 'never tells wives that they are to love their husbands . . . The reason is that which he gives: Christ loves the church, but it is for the church to obey and submit to Christ' (C. Chavasse cited by R. P. Martin).

CHAPTER SIX

Here further guidance is given on family relationships. Paul exhorts children to obey their parents, and he tells fathers to exercise restraint in the nurture of their children [vv 1–4]. Slaves are to regard their work as a service to Christ, while masters must avoid threatening since their heavenly Master shows no partiality in his judgments [vv 5–9]. The final exhortation is a rousing call to prepare for battle. Believers must put on the whole armour of God in order to stand against the powers of darkness which oppose them [vv 10–17]. The apostle requests his readers to pray that he may be given boldness to preach the mystery of the gospel, and urges them to continue in prayer for all the saints. He warmly commends his messenger Tychicus, and closes the Epistle with the benediction [vv 18–24].

*V*1: **Children, obey your parents in the Lord: for this is right.** Paul next deals with the mutual duties of children and parents [vv 1–4]. His use of the phrase 'in the Lord' makes the natural obligation of children to obey their parents a summons to religious service. They are to recognize that in obeying their parents, they are obeying Christ. 'Not merely natural instinct, but religious motive should prompt children to obedience, and guard them in it ... Filial obedience is "right"; it has its foundation in the very essence of that relation which subsists between parents and children. Nature claims it, while

Scripture enjoins it, and the Son of God exemplified it.'
(Eadie) [*Luke* 2.51].

*V*2: **Honour thy father and mother (which is the first
commandment with promise),**
*V*3: **that it may be well with thee, and thou mayest live
long on the earth.**

**'Honour thy father and mother,' which is a command-
ment of the greatest importance with a promise attached** (Arndt-Gingrich). Paul confirms this injunction by
an appeal to the abiding authority of the moral law [*Exod*
20.12; *Deut* 5.16], while he makes the promise universal in
its scope by taking away the local reference to Canaan – an
inspired adaptation that teaches us to distinguish the enduring
substance of the moral law from the historical *accidents* that belonged to its Old Testament form. Thus each child must
honour father and mother as worthy of equal respect and
obedience. This is a commandment of primary importance
to which is attached the promise of a long and blessed life.
'Obedient children sometimes die, as ripe fruit falls first. But
the promise of longevity is held out – it is a principle of the
divine administration and the usual course of providence . . .
Filial obedience, under God's blessing, prolongs life, for it
implies the possession of principles of restraint, sobriety, and
industry, which secure a lengthened existence' (Eadie) [cf
Prov 10.27].

*V*4: **And, ye fathers, provoke not your children to
wrath: but nurture them in the chastening and admonition of the Lord.**

On the other hand, fathers (upon whom the responsibility for
the family primarily rests) also have a duty towards their
children. This 'is given first *negatively*, as avoidance of all

calculated to *irritate* or *exasperate* the children – injustice, severity and the like, so as to make them indisposed to filial obedience and honour' (Salmond).

but bring them up in the discipline and instruction of the Lord. (RSV) Paul's *positive* directive to fathers is that they are to train their children in the *Christian* way, giving them 'the training that is of Christ, proceeding from him and prescribed by him' (Salmond). This means that fathers are not only to treat their children fairly but also firmly; repressive harshness and weak indulgence are alike to be avoided [cf 1 Sam 3.13]. Rather they are to guide them by discipline and instruction. *Discipline* is 'the training by act' which Trench refers to 'the laws and ordinances of the Christian household, the transgression of which will induce correction'; whereas *instruction* is 'the training by word – by the word of encouragement, when this is sufficient, but also by that of remonstrance, of reproof, of blame, where these may be required'.

V5: **Servants, be obedient unto them that according to the flesh are your masters, with fear and trembling, in singleness of your heart, as unto Christ;**

It is because Paul's 'household code' is based on the general principle stated in 5.21 that he first speaks to those in a position of dependence, wives, children, and now *servants* [*vv* 5–8], before dealing with those who are placed in authority over them, husbands, fathers, and *masters* [*v* 9]. Although many modern versions rightly translate 'slaves', it is perhaps preferable to retain 'servants' because the exhortation 'embodies principles applicable to all posts of subordination' (Simpson). If Paul had preached 'the social gospel' he doubtless would have encouraged slaves to repudiate their position, with disastrous consequences, yet in sending the converted slave Onesimus back to his master as 'a brother beloved' [*Philemon*

v 16] he set forth the great principle of religious equality before God which undermined and eventually brought about
the abolition of slavery. So here the apostle asks for that heart-
obedience which only the redeemed man is able to render to
his master. As the adoption of this ethic led to a transformation of the slave/master relationship, so its widespread absence
from the modern industrial scene is diagnosed by John Murray
as 'our basic economic ill' (*Principles of Conduct*, p. 103).

with fear and trembling, Not in servile fear of man, but in
the fear of God. Christian slaves 'were not to tremble lest anything unpleasant might happen to themselves, but lest their
Lord's name should be brought into disrepute through them'
(Bruce).

in singleness of your heart, as unto Christ; Paul insists
that it is the duty of servants always to obey their earthly
masters with conscientious care and sincerity of purpose, as
those who are well assured that in so doing they are serving
their heavenly Master [cf *Col* 3.22–24].

*V*6: **not in the way of eyeservice, as men-pleasers; but
as servants of Christ, doing the will of God from the
heart;**
*V*7: **with good will doing service, as unto the Lord,
and not unto men:**

not in the way of eyeservice, as men-pleasers; 'The vice
was venial in slaves; it is inexcusable, because it darkens into
theft, in paid servants; and it spreads far and wide. All scam-
ped work, all productions of man's hand and brain which are
got up to look better than they are, all fussy parade of diligence
when under inspection, and slackness afterwards, and all their
like, which infect and infest every trade and profession, are

transfixed by the sharp point of this precept' (Alexander Maclaren).

but as servants of Christ, doing the will of God from the heart; This is the antidote for such shoddy service. When the worker regards himself as the bond-slave of Christ his work is always well done. For the most humdrum job becomes a vocation when it is looked upon as the doing of God's will.

with good will doing service, as unto the Lord, and not unto men. No labour is servile when the Lord's approval is the paramount consideration. The most willing service to men is rendered by those who are bent on pleasing Christ!

*V*8: **knowing that whatsoever good thing each one doeth, the same shall he receive again from the Lord, whether *he be* bond or free.**

'This verse presents for the encouragement of the slave, the elevating truth that all men stand on a level before the bar of Christ . . . In this world some men are masters and some are slaves. In the next, these distinctions will cease. There the question will be, not, Who is the master? and Who the slave? but who has done the will of God?' (Charles Hodge). Thus in the day of judgment every believer will be rewarded according to the good that he has done [the converse truth is stated in *Col* 3.25]. And as every good work is the fruit of grace, so the promised reward is also the reward of grace.

*V*9: **And, ye masters, do the same things unto them, and forbear threatening: knowing that he who is both their Master and yours is in heaven, and there is no respect of persons with him.**

And, ye masters, do the same things unto them, 'Perform your reciprocal duty' (Calvin). For masters are also under an obligation to their servants [cf *Col* 4.1: 'that which is just and equal']. 'This is what Paul means by the term "the same things"; for we are all ready enough to demand what is due to ourselves; but when our own duty comes to be performed, every one tries to plead exemption' (Calvin).

giving up your threatening 'Your' is literally 'the' – the article hinting at its common occurrence: 'the too habitual threatening'. Paul 'singles out the prevailing vice and most customary exhibition of bad feeling on the part of the master, and in forbidding this naturally includes every similar form of harshness' (Ellicott).

knowing that he who is both their Master and yours is in heaven, and that there is no partiality with him. (RSV) This heavenly Master 'is not a judge who "takes the face", sees who a man is and decides his case with partiality, in favour of the one who is a lord and master, rich and powerful, in disfavour of one who is a poor slave and powerless' (Lenski) [*James* 5.1ff].

*V*10: **Finally, be strong in the Lord, and in the strength of his might.**

As in 1.19 with which this verse is vitally connected, the final phrase is not to be reduced to 'in his mighty strength', but has the full force of 'in the active efficacy of the might that is inherent in him' (Salmond). Paul now draws the Epistle to its practical conclusion. He charges his readers to stand fast against all the powers of evil, acquitting themselves like soldiers who are divinely strengthened and equipped to engage in this conflict [*vv* 10–20]. This command is of primary necessity, for the finest armour is wasted on the soldier who has no will to fight. And as the armour is spiritual, so is this courage; 'for physical courage and intellectual prowess are often, alas! allied to spiritual cowardice. Moreover, soldiers have an invincible courage when they have confidence in the skill and bravery of their leader; and the power of his might, in which they are strong, has proved its vigour in routing the same foes which they are summoned to encounter. As the Captain of salvation, "He spoiled principalities and powers, and triumphed over them" ' (Eadie) [*Col* 2.15].

V11: Put on the whole armour of God, that ye may be able to stand against the wiles of the devil.

Put on the whole armour To be fully furnished for the fight the Christian must put on the *whole* armour of God. '*He must be armed, in every part* cap-à-pie, *soul and body*, the powers of the one, and the senses of the other, not any part left naked. A dart may fly in at a little hole, like that which brought a message of death to Ahab, through the joints of his harness, and Satan is such an archer, who can shoot at penny-breadth' (William Gurnall) [cf *Rom* 13.12, 14].

of God, This is the armour that *God* provides; it is not of man's devising. 'Instead of relying on the arms which God has provided, men have always been disposed to trust to those which they provide for themselves or which have been prescribed by others. Seclusion from the world (i.e. flight rather than conflict), ascetic and ritual observances, invocation of saints and angels, and especially, celibacy, voluntary poverty, and monastic obedience, constitute the panoply which false religion has substituted for the armour of God' (Charles Hodge) [cf *Col* 2.18–23].

that ye may be able to stand ' "To stand" is the key-word of the passage. The present picture is not of a march, or of an assault, but of the holding of the fortress of the soul and of the church for the heavenly King. Bunyan's "Mr Standfast" is a portrait that may illustrate this page' (Moule, *CB*) [cf *vv* 13, 14].

against the wiles of the devil. All the resources of divine grace are required to stand firm against the prince of darkness, an adversary of superhuman strength and guile, whose greatest triumph is to make men doubt his existence! The devil 'useth arts and stratagems, as well as force and violence, and therefore, if any part of your spiritual armour be wanting, he will assault you where he finds you weakest' (Poole). [cf 4.14; 2 *Cor* 11.3, 13, 14].

*V*12: **For our wrestling is not against flesh and blood, but against the principalities, against the powers, against the world-rulers of this darkness, against the spiritual *hosts* of wickedness in the heavenly *places*.**

It is because the forces arrayed against believers are not merely human opponents, men of flesh and blood like themselves, but the massed legions of the evil one, that they must put on the whole armour of God. And to show the absolute necessity for this divine provision, Paul, as it were, parades the devil's army in review, using each of the four designations to set forth a different aspect of this dreadful host. The term 'principalities' is probably meant to indicate that these fallen angels have retained the rank of ruling dignitaries. That this is no empty title is shown by the fact that these rebellious spirits are also called 'powers', which suggests that they are invested with the authority to exercise such rule. The third phrase defines the sphere of their dominion: the world in its present state of darkness is the realm over which they exert their usurped sway within the limits permitted them [cf *Dan* 10.13, 20]. Finally, 'the spirit-forces of evil' (Moffatt) points to an invisible horde whose 'appetite for evil only exceeds their capacity for producing it' (Eadie). The domain of this army appears to be located in a region above the earth but below the highest heavens [cf 2.2]. The reason why Paul uses 'in the heavenlies' and not 'in the air' here may be his wish to 'bring out *as strongly as possible* the superhuman and superterrestrial nature of these hostile spirits' (Meyer).

*V*13: **Wherefore take up the whole armour of God, that ye may be able to withstand in the evil day, and, having done all, to stand.**

Since Christians must contend against such formidable adversaries, it is essential that they take up the 'panoply' (i.e. 'the full armour of a heavily armed soldier' – Arndt-Gingrich) of God.

> *Stand then in his great might,*
> *With all his strength endued;*
> *And take, to arm you for the fight,*
> *The panoply of God.*
> Charles Wesley

that ye may be able to withstand in the evil day, [cf 5.16] The Christian soldier must be thoroughly prepared in order that he may be able to withstand any sudden assault that is launched against him. 'The evil day' is the day when the conflict is most severe. It is any day of which it can be said 'This is your hour, and the power of darkness' [*Luke* 22.53].

and, having done all, Some maintain that the meaning is, '*after* proving victorious over everything' (Arndt-Gingrich). But '*after you have done* or *accomplished everything*' (Arndt-Gingrich) in preparing for the battle is preferable. For it is unlikely that Paul would first speak of the result of the combat and then urge his readers to put on the armour piece by piece [*vv* 14–17].

to stand. The central idea of the passage is not progress or conquest, but that of standing firm in the faith. 'The scene is filled with the marshalled hosts of the Evil One, bent upon *dislodging* the soul, and the church, from the one possible vantage-ground of life and power – union and communion with their Lord' (Moule, *CB*).

*V*14: **Stand therefore, having girded your loins with truth, and having put on the breastplate of righteousness,**

In order that the Christian soldier may take his stand in readiness for the fight, he must first have put on the complete armour of God, which Paul now enumerates.

1. He must brace himself with the belt of truth, which most commentators, including Calvin, take to be sincerity of heart. This subjective interpretation is inadequate because not even Christian virtues constitute the armour that God provides. Nothing less than the objective realities of the gospel will afford the believer the divine protection he requires to resist the devil's wiles. Accordingly, 'truth' is to be understood as the dependable reality that has come to us in the gospel [cf *John* 14.6]. This 'is something which the believer can put on like the protective apron of the soldier. He can make active use of it in withstanding the assaults of evil' (A. Oepke, *TDNT*, Vol. V, p. 308).

2. He must put on the breastplate of righteousness, which in view of the ethical context is also generally explained in the subjective sense of living righteously. 'But this is no protection. It cannot resist the accusations of conscience, the whispers of despondency, the power of temptation, much less the severity of the law, or the assaults of Satan. What Paul desired for himself was not to have on his own righteousness, but the

righteousness which is of God by faith [*Phil* 3.8, 9]. And this, doubtless, is the righteousness which he here urges believers to put on as a breastplate. It is an infinitely perfect righteousness, consisting in the obedience and sufferings of the Son of God, which satisfies all the demands of the divine law and justice; and which is a sure defence against all assaults whether from within or from without' (Charles Hodge).

*V*15: **and having shod your feet with the preparation of the gospel of peace;**

and have your feet shod with the stability of the gospel of peace, (Moffatt). 3. Here again opinion is divided on the meaning of the word 'preparation', which may refer to a readiness to preach the gospel [*Is* 52.7]; but in the Greek version of *Ps* 88.15 [*Ps* 89.14 in our versions] it has the sense of a 'prepared foundation', and this is more in harmony with the idea of standing unmoved against the foe. So if we would have a 'firm footing' (NEB) for the fight, we must put on these heavily-studded shoes of the gospel of peace [cf 2.14ff]. Thus we are prepared for the war with Satan by the realization of our peace with God! Such peace does not exempt us from active service, but rather sustains us in it. For as no soldier stands firm in the day of battle unless his morale is high, so believers must be assured of their acceptance with God before they can withstand the assaults of the great adversary of their souls [*Rom* 5.1].

*V*16: **withal taking up the shield of faith, wherewith ye shall be able to quench all the fiery darts of the evil** *one*.

4. 'In addition to all' the believer must take up the shield of faith. Here the protection afforded the heavy infantryman by the large, oblong shield, four by two and a half feet, is likened to the faith with which the Christian is able to quench all the

flaming missiles that are hurled at him by the tempter. This faith is neither self-generated (carnal self-confidence) nor reflexive (faith in our faith), but is the gift of God (cf 2.8) by which we are enabled to lay hold of Christ and all his saving benefits. It is therefore a faith which is as objective as the shield with which it is compared. The subjective aspect of faith is covered by the command to take up and use this shield in quenching all the devil's fire-tipped darts.

'As burning arrows not only pierced but set on fire what they pierced, they were doubly dangerous. They serve here therefore as the symbol of the fierce onsets of Satan. He showers arrows of fire on the soul of the believer; who, if unprotected by the shield of faith, would soon perish. It is a common experience of the people of God that at times horrible thoughts, unholy, blasphemous, sceptical, malignant, crowd upon the mind, which cannot be accounted for on any ordinary law of mental action, and which cannot be dislodged. They stick like burning arrows; and fill the soul with agony. They can be quenched only by faith; by calling on Christ for help. These, however, are not the only kind of fiery darts; nor are they the most dangerous. There are others which enkindle passion, inflame ambition, excite cupidity, pride, discontent, or vanity; producing a flame which our deceitful heart is not so prompt to extinguish, and which is often allowed to burn until it produces great injury and even destruction. Against these most dangerous weapons of the evil one, the only protection is faith. It is only by looking to Christ and earnestly invoking his interposition in our behalf that we can resist these insidious assaults, which inflame evil without the warning of pain' (Charles Hodge).

V17: **And take the helmet of salvation, and the sword of the Spirit, which is the word of God:**

5. In this case Paul uses a different verb which specifically indicates (though not in contrast to the other pieces of armour)

that the helmet of salvation is to be 'received' as a gift from God. As in verse 14 the apostle evidently has in mind *Is* 59.17, where God is depicted as the Warrior who 'wears the helmet of salvation as the Worker and Bringer of salvation' (Foulkes). This is therefore the helmet of victory, for we receive it as an objective assurance that the decisive battle has been already fought and won on our behalf. So in putting in on we are subjectively trusting in that salvation which is at once given and promised, which is ours both in present possession and future prospect [cf 1 *Thess* 5.8]. And since it is the function of the helmet to protect the soldier's head and ensure his clear vision through its visor, so this 'given' salvation must fill the Christian's mind and keep his eyes fixed upon the glorious goal that is set before him. We must at all times remember the objective character of God's salvation, and not become un-healthily obsessed with our own subjective spiritual states. We have to preserve the balance Luther showed in his great hymn, 'A safe stronghold our God is still', which though it speaks of his experience, puts the whole emphasis on the out-ward and upward, upon God (cf James Philip's brilliant and heart-warming exposition in *The Christian Warfare and Armour* pp. 83–97).

and the sword of the Spirit which is the spoken word of God, (Hendriksen). 6. The only offensive weapon in the Christian's armoury is the sword of the Spirit, which is identified with the Word of God [cf *Heb* 4.12]. For it is only by this means that the powers of darkness are put to flight. What is in view is the special utterance of God that is exactly fitted to repel the tempter's attack on any particular occasion. Just as Christ routed the devil by appealing to particular texts of Scripture [cf *Matt* 4.4, 7, 10], so the Christian must learn to wield the sword of the Spirit with such effect that he is able to parry all the deadly thrusts of the enemy. 'All scripture is given by inspiration of God' [2 *Tim* 3.16], but it is only through knowing it for ourselves that it becomes the sword of the Spirit in our hands. The Christian is invincible when armed with this Excalibur whose power belongs to the Spirit who inspired it; yet it is he and no one else who is commanded to do the fighting! Unhappily, many are now using the Bible as a sword to do the devil's work in the world. The aggressive cultists of our day are not taught of the Spirit, but simply come to Scripture for the authority to propagate the ideas they wish to impose upon the sacred text. So in their case the Word of God is the sword upon which they commit spiritual suicide, taking down their deluded followers with them into the pit! [*Rev* 22.18, 19].

*V*18: **with all prayer and supplication praying at all seasons in the Spirit, and watching thereunto in all perseverance and supplication for all the saints.**

7. This state of spiritual preparedness ['Stand therefore', *v* 14] would not be complete without the weapon of 'all-prayer', and though Paul now drops the metaphor he clearly wishes his readers to understand that persevering prayer [*Luke* 18.1] is essential to the success of this warfare.

> *Restraining prayer, we cease to fight;*
> *Prayer makes the Christian's armour bright;*
> *And Satan trembles when he sees*
> *The weakest saint upon his knees.*
> William Cowper.

in the Spirit, [cf *Jude v* 20] This is added because 'true prayer is both the suitor's own and the Spirit's work. The sincerity and intension of soul pertain to the human petitioner; the potency, inspiration and freedom of utterance and access [2.18] spring from "the secret touch of the Spirit" (Gurnall),

generating a glow of holy emotion in the suppliant's soul'
(Simpson).

**and watching thereunto in all perseverance and suppli-
cation for all the saints,** 'The conflict of which the apostle
has been speaking is not merely a single combat between the
individual Christian and Satan, but also a war between the
people of God and the powers of darkness. No soldier entering
battle prays for himself alone, but for all his fellow-soldiers
also. They form one army, and the success of the one is the
success of all. In like manner Christians are united as one army,
and therefore have a common cause; and each must pray for
all' (Charles Hodge).

*V*19: **and on my behalf, that utterance may be given
unto me in opening my mouth, to make known with
boldness the mystery of the gospel,**

Although an apostle, Paul was always careful to ask his
fellow-believers to pray for him, and here he requests them
to pray that God will speak through his lips, enabling him
boldly to proclaim 'the mystery of the gospel' [for which see
comment on 3.9]. 'Like the early apostles [*Acts* 4.29] his prayer
was not for success, nor for deliverance from danger or suffering, but for boldness in proclaiming the gospel of God that
was entrusted to him' (Foulkes).

*V*20: **for which I am an ambassador in chains; that in it
I may speak boldly, as I ought to speak.**

for which I am an ambassador in a chain; (ASV margin)
[cf 2 *Cor* 5.20] 'Ambassadors were inviolable by the law of
nations, and could not, without outrage to sacred right, be
put in chains. Yet Christ's ambassador is in *a chain*!' (Fausset).
Pending the hearing of his appeal to Caesar Paul was allowed

to hire his own lodging in Rome, but was kept chained to the soldier who guarded him [*Acts* 28.16, 20].

that I may declare it boldly, as I ought to speak. (RSV) 'It' meaning the message of the gospel [cf *Col* 4.4]. Thus Paul invokes their prayers on his behalf that he may fearlessly discharge his commission despite his chain [cf *Acts* 28.30, 31].

*V*21: **But that ye also may know my affairs, how I do, Tychicus, the beloved brother and faithful minister in the Lord, shall make known to you all things:**
*V*22: **whom I have sent unto you for this very purpose, that ye may know our state, and that he may comfort your hearts.**

The close verbal similarity of this personal postscript with that found in *Col* 4.7, 8 is best explained 'by the supposition that the apostle wrote the two conclusions together, when both letters had been written and were about to be despatched' (Foulkes). For after having addressed the Colossians it would be natural for Paul to add the word 'also' when virtually repeating the same message to the Ephesians. The bearer of these epistles and of all the news from Rome is Tychicus [*Acts* 20.4], Paul's beloved brother and faithful helper 'in the Lord', whose ministry is certain to encourage and strengthen their hearts.

*V*23: **Peace be to the brethren, and love with faith, from God the Father and the Lord Jesus Christ.**

As Paul writes to those who are believers, his closing prayer for them is that their faith may be accompanied by the graces of peace and love. 'It is evident that the peace here intended is peace among themselves as brethren, and that love is not the love of God manifested toward them, but the Christian grace of brotherly love, which is the only true basis of peace in the community' (Macpherson). And the apostle makes this the subject of prayer because such graces will not be manifested on the horizontal level unless they descend from heaven as blessings conjointly bestowed by God the Father and the Lord Jesus Christ.

*V*24: **Grace be with all them that love our Lord Jesus Christ with *a love* incorruptible.**

It is with this beautiful benediction that the great apostle fittingly concludes his 'spiritual testament' to the church. 'The benediction is upon those who love Christ with an incorruptible love. They love him who first loved them; and this love, which they have experienced and which has produced their love, has imparted to them and to their love that same incorruptibility which belongs to him and to his love. Their love is not of the earth earthly. It is heavenly, of heavenly origin and of heavenly quality. That love which is of Christ and in Christ can know no decay' (Macpherson).

Soli Deo Gloria

BIBLIOGRAPHY

BIBLIOGRAPHY AND ACKNOWLEDGEMENTS

Quotations have been selected from the following books, and the author expresses his grateful thanks to the authors and publishers who have kindly given permission to reproduce quotations from their copyright works.

Abbott, T. K., *The Epistle to the Ephesians and to the Colossians* (ICC) (T & T Clark, 1897)

Berkouwer, G. C., *Faith and Justification* (Eerdmans, 1972)

Bruce, F. F., *The Epistle to the Ephesians* (Pickering & Inglis, 1961)

Bruce, F. F., *An Expanded Paraphrase on the Epistles of Paul* (Paternoster Press, 1970)

Calvin, John, *Commentary on Ephesians*, translated by T. H. L. Parker, (St. Andrew Press, 1965)

Denney, James, *The Death of Christ* (Tyndale, 1964)

Eadie, John, *Commentary on the Epistle to the Ephesians* (Zondervan reprint of 1883 ed.)

Ellicott, C. J., *St. Paul's Epistle to the Ephesians* (Longmans Green, 1868)

Fausset, A. R., *Ephesians* (JFB) (Collins, 1874)

Findlay, G. G., *The Epistle to the Ephesians* (EB) (Hodder & Stoughton, 1892)

Foulkes, Francis, *Ephesians – Introduction and Commentary* (TNTC) (Tyndale Press, 1963)

Geldenhuys, J. Norval, *Supreme Authority* (Marshall, Morgan & Scott, 1953)

Goodwin, Thomas, *Exposition of Ephesians* (1–2.10) (Sovereign Grace Book Club, nd)

Gurnall, William, *The Christian in Complete Armour* (The Banner of Truth, 1964)

Hanson, Stig, *The Unity of the Church in the New Testament – Colossians and Ephesians* (Almquist & Wiksells, 1946)

Henry, Matthew, *Commentary on the Holy Bible* (various editions)

Hodge, A. A., *The Atonement* (Evangelical Press, 1974)

Hodge, Charles, *Commentary on Ephesians* (The Banner of Truth, 1964)

Hoeksema, Herman, *Reformed Dogmatics* (Reformed Free Publishing, 1966)

Hoeksema, Herman, *The Triple Knowledge* (Reformed Free Publishing, 1966)

Kidner, Derek, *Genesis* (TOTC) (Tyndale, 1967)

Kidner, Derek, *Psalms 1–72* (TOTC) (Tyndale, 1973)

Kittel, Gerhard and Friedrich, Gerhard (Editors), *Theological Dictionary of the New Testament*, Vols. 1–9 (Eerdmans, 1964–1974) translated by Geoffrey W. Bromiley)

Lenski, R. C. H., *The Interpretation of Ephesians* (Augsburg, 1961)

Lightfoot, J. B., *Notes on the Epistles of St. Paul* (Zondervan, 1957)

Lightfoot, J. B., *Colossians and Philemon* (Zondervan, 1961)

Lightfoot, J. B., *Philippians* (Zondervan, 1968)

McKelvey, R. J., *The New Temple* (OUP, 1969)

Mcpherson, John, *Commentary on Ephesians* (T & T Clark, 1892)

Machen, J. G., *The Christian Faith in the Modern World* (Eerdmans, 1970)

Manton, Thomas, *Exposition of John XVII* (The Banner of Truth, 1959)

Martin, Ralph P., *Ephesians* (NBC) (IVP, 1970)

Martin, Ralph P., *Worship in the Early Church* (Marshall, Morgan & Scott 1974)

Morris, Leon, *The Apostolic Preaching of the Cross* (Tyndale, 1965)

Moule, C. F. D., *An Idiom-Book of New Testament Greek* (CUP, 1968)

Moule, H. C. G., *The Epistle to the Ephesians* (CB) (CUP, 1889)

Moule, H. C. G., *Ephesian Studies* (Pickering & Inglis, nd)

Murray, John *Principles of Conduct* (Tyndale, 1957)

Pink, Arthur W., *Gleanings from Paul* (Moody Press, 1967)

Poole, Matthew, *A Commentary on the Holy Bible*, Vol. III (The Banner of Truth, 1963)

Richardson, Alan (Editor), *A Theological Word Book of the Bible* (SCM, 1957)

BIBLIOGRAPHY AND ACKNOWLEDGEMENTS

Robinson, J. Armitage, *St. Paul's Epistle to the Ephesians* (James Clarke, n.d.)

Salmond, S. D. F., *The Epistle to the Ephesians* (EGT) (Hodder & Stoughton 1903)

Simpson, E. K., *The Epistle to the Ephesians* (NLC) (Marshall, Morgan & Scott, 1957)

Stott, John, *Baptism and Fullness* (IVP, 1975)

Thornwell, James Henley, *The Collected Writings,* Vol. II (The Banner of Truth, 1974)

Trapp, John, *Commentary on the New Testament* (Sovereign Grace Book Club, 1958)

Trench, R. C., *Synonyms of the New Testament* (James Clarke, 1961)

Vincent, M. R., *Word Studies in the New Testament* (MacDonald, nd)

Vos, Geerhardus, *The Pauline Eschatology* (Eerdmans, 1961)

Warfield, B. B., *The Shorter Writings*, Vol. I. (edited by John E. Meeter) (Presbyterian & Reformed, 1970)

IN ADDITION TO THESE THE FOLLOWING BOOKS WERE CONSULTED:

Alford, Henry, *The Greek Testament* (Rivingtons, 1859)

Arndt, W. F. and Gingrich, F. W., *A Greek English Lexicon of the New Testament* (University of Chicago Press, 1957)

Barth, Markus, *Ephesians* (AB) (Doubleday, 1974)

Best, Ernest, *One Body in Christ* (SPCK, 1955)

Calvin, John *Sermons on the Epistle to the Ephesians* (Banner of Truth, 1973)

Clowney, Edmund P., *The Doctrine of the Church* (Presbyterian & Reformed 1969)

Dabney, R. L., *Lectures on Systematic Theology* (Zondervan, 1972)

Dunn, James D. G., *Baptism in the Holy Spirit* (SCM, 1970)

Guthrie, Donald, *New Testament Introduction* (Tyndale, 1970)

Hendriksen, William, *Ephesians* (NTC) (The Banner of Truth, 1972)

Lloyd-Jones, D. M., *God's Way of Reconciliation* (Evangelical Press, 1972)

Lloyd-Jones, D. M., *Life in the Spirit* (The Banner of Truth, 1974)

Lloyd-Jones, D. M., *The Christian Warfare* (The Banner of Truth, 1976)

MacDonald, H. D., *The Church and its Glory* (Henry Walter, 1973)

Martin, Ralph P., *Ephesians* (BBC) (Marshall, Morgan & Scott, 1972)

BIBLIOGRAPHY AND ACKNOWLEDGEMENTS

Mitton, C. Leslie, *Ephesians* (NCB) (Oliphants, 1976)

Murray, J. O. F., *The Epistle to the Ephesians* (CGT) (CUP, 1889)

Philip, James, *The Christian Warfare and Armour* (Victory Press, 1972)

Thayer, J. H., *A Greek-English Lexicon of the New Testament* (Evangel Publishing, 1974)

Thomas, L. R., *Does the Bible teach Millenialism?* (Reiner Publications, nd)

Warfield, B. B., *The Person and Work of Christ* (Presbyterian & Reformed 1950)

Warfield, B. B., *The Lord of Glory* (Evangelical Press, 1974)

Warfield, B. B., *Faith and Life* (Banner of Truth, 1974)